MW00379777

In her debut book, Unfrozen, Andrea Wenburg gently takes the reader on a journey of discovering their true voice by telling the story of how she found hers. The pain of not feeling heard was palpable. I cheered her on through the very last chapter, and the last sentence was so satisfying to me as a reader. I recommend this book to anyone who needs to find their true voice so they can be heard in this very noisy world.

- Anna LaBaron
  Author of The Polygamist's Daughter

A genuine, heart-baring, and inspirational autobiography about a woman's battle with self-imposed expectations. A recommended read for anyone afraid to be imperfect in front of themselves, others, or God.

- Espen Klausen, Ph.D.
  Licensed Psychologist and Public Speaker

Unfrozen would be a fantastic read for both adults and teenagers alike, and a great resource for parents and youth leaders to utilize with teens and young adults as well as women's ministry programs.

- Christina Klausen, MA
  Resource Center Coordinator, Community Church Fond du Lac

If you want to experience freedom from the fickle whims of the world around you, read Unfrozen for an inspiring story of one woman's journey of soaring through childhood dreams, stumbling through young adult relational struggles, precariously balancing the expectations of a new marriage, being battered by the trauma of childbirth, learning to walk in the path of self-acceptance, and finally, soaring into self-offering.

- Kili Wenburg, MA
  Spiritual Director

How refreshing! An imperfect author! Andrea's raw reveal gives integrity to her infectious invitation. It turns out that God has chosen, loved, and released only the truly flawed, but uniquely fascinating, image-bearers to give voice to His love!

- Neal Brower, MDiv, LLD
  Pastor, Author, EFCA District Superintendent

With a spunky sense of unshrinking spirit, Andrea tells us her story in UNFROZEN, of discovering her voice in the context of the greater dialog of life.

Relating intimately to the snow queen Elsa and her sister Anna in the movie "FROZEN", she invites us to thoughtfully consider how perpetual self protection and preservation often circumvent meaningful conversations and relationships, then points the way to liberate true love.

As Andrea offers her voice, her gift, to the world, her act of true love on behalf of others, she invites each of us to as well.

- Kimberlye Berg
  Author of *Schema of a Soul*

Unfrozen reminded me that I wasn't alone in holding back parts of myself out of fear. It reignited my courage to release my true voice and message into the world in a bigger way. What a powerful book!

- Holly Mthethwa
  Author of *Hot Chocolate in June: A True Story of Loss, Love and Restoration*

UNFROZEN

Stop Holding Back and Release The Real You

. . .

The unexpected path to connected relationships
and extraordinary impact

ANDREA JOY WENBURG

Unfrozen: Stop Holding Back and Release the Real You

Copyright © 2016 Andrea Joy Wenburg

Uprising Press

Edited by Rosanne Moore

Cover design by Ida Sveningsson
Formatting by Janelle Reed

For my true love
Aaron

CONTENTS

SECTION THREE: Hiding the Real Me

SECTION FOUR: Releasing the Real Me

Note to the Reader

August, 2016
Dear Reader,

A few short years ago, I wasn't sure I could face the thoughts and feelings I feared might lurk in the deeper places of my soul. So I avoided the quiet and numbed my tender heart with distractions. But I wasn't satisfied. I was stuck and I wanted a way out.

If that's you, then you're in the right place. I wrote this book for you.

I'm offering you the opportunity to come with me on a journey as I struggle to make sense of my identity and voice of self-expression in my relationships with God, my husband and the world. I'm extending my hand and inviting you to come along because I know that there is freedom, empowerment and abundant love waiting on the other side.

But many people find the unexpected path to be a challenging one.

With that in mind, I've created a set of free companion videos and discussion guide to support you as you read and process your interaction with the book.

Go to http://andreajoywenburg.com to enter the Unfrozen Resource Center and discover what I have prepared for you. Then invite your daughter (10+), a younger woman, a small group of friends or your spouse to join you in authentic heart-level discussion.

I hope you're up for the challenge because your frozen heart is worth mining.

Finally Unfrozen,
Andrea Joy

PROLOGUE

"I've got a lot of work to do," Aaron sighed. We were nearly home from spending Thanksgiving weekend with family.

"I know."

As we prepared to pull off the interstate, I looked out the window at the Nebraska prairie whizzing past. He always had work to do. I'd spent the past three years taking care of our kids while Aaron attempted to dig out of the paperwork hole he'd fallen into as a small business owner. It wasn't something we could do anything about, and I felt bad for him, but... *How will I ever get myself out of this hole as long as he is in his?*

"What are we going to do when we get home, Mom? Can we play with friends?" I glanced back at our 6-year-old Amelia. Her intense need to have our schedule planned out in her head made it difficult for me to feel like I was ever on top of things.

"No. Today isn't a friend day."

"Well, what fun thing are we going to do?!"

My muscles wound tight as she spoke, and then I glanced at Grant. His little body looked as tired as I felt. Grant spent the first four years of his life waking up at 4:00 a.m. Chronic sleep deprivation threatened to strangle the life out of me. I probably looked like it. Fortunately, we were at a point in Grant's life when I didn't have to wake up with him every morning, but I was still tired. Oh, so tired.

The truth was, I was also angry. It seemed like my kids, my husband, our dogs and even God were in on this conspiracy to keep me awake and on edge. I simply couldn't catch up. Just as soon as I began to feel rested, someone had a bad dream or needed me when I went to sleep. I didn't like having to fight for my sanity, but what choice did I have? If I didn't, I was utterly defeated on most days by 7 AM.

My consolation was that we could afford a few distractions. "I think I'll take the kids to the new Disney movie this afternoon while you work." The thought of theater popcorn and a large Coke took the edge off the disappointment of another lonely Sunday.

"OK." He looked at me apologetically and then pulled into our garage.

Leaving the kids in the car, I slipped into the house, through the laundry room and into our kitchen. I opened the pantry door to grab our popcorn bucket, but it was full of mismatched lids and containers. Dumping it out onto the shelf, I shut the door and sighed.

I'll get them later.

I shook away the acknowledgment that I had no intention of cleaning up my mess. Looking around our expansive kitchen, I mused again at how empty it felt...about as empty as I was.

"We'll be back in a couple of hours," Tears threatened to spill out as Aaron kissed me goodbye. I felt like a shell of the vibrant woman who married him 8 years before. While I wasn't depressed, I wasn't happy either. I wasn't sure what I was.

A few minutes later I shooed Amelia and Grant into the crowded concession line at the movie theater. Glancing down, I saw Grant lying on the ground. "Grant! Stand up!"

No matter how early he'd gotten up that morning, I didn't want to have to hold him while we stood in line for popcorn.

I looked at my adorable kids and shook my head. A couple of days earlier, Amelia told me she was tired because Grant was waking her up at 5:00 a.m. every morning. I was incredulous: "Why?!"

"He just wants to play," she told me.

No wonder they are fighting by 11:00 a.m. every day! If only there were a simple way to get more sleep...

"Mo-om!" Amelia insisted I come out of my head and back into the concession line. "What time is it?" She was the most time-aware 6-year-old child I knew. "What time does the movie start?! We're going to be late!"

"Shhh. We'll be fine." I scowled. Having my thoughts interrupted irritated me, and I had no intention of going into this movie without popcorn.

There had been a time when I watched grown-up movies to stimulate creativity and intellectual analysis. Now I went to children's movies with the kids, hoping I wouldn't poke my eyes out with boredom. And that's why we're not skipping the popcorn.

A few minutes later, we found seats in the front of the theater and started stuffing kernels into our mouths by the handful. I heaved a big sigh, wondering what the movie was going to be about. Based on the trailer, I expected Disney's *Frozen* to be nothing but a fluffy children's movie about a cute snowman and a reindeer.

The movie began and my disgruntled musings about my sleep-woes were interrupted by ethereal vocal sounds. I looked up to see Cinderella's castle transitioning into the snowy dark of night and one big, bright, beautifully complicated snowflake.

Cocking my head to the side, I squinted. The dark mountainous landscape developing before my eyes seemed anything but fluffy. Out of nowhere, wide-toothed saws ripped through the mountain lake ice, and a chorus of men's voices declared the dangers of a frozen heart.

I hadn't anticipated a musical. I love musicals!

Soon, a castle near the mouth of a fjord appeared. Inside the castle, Anna jumped on her sister Elsa, as Elsa lay sleeping in bed. And then little Anna asked Elsa if she wanted to build a snowman. The sisters appeared to be the same ages as Grant and Amelia. Their playful, early morning innocence cut through my icy exterior as violently as the sawing in the first scene. *How did they know?*

Quiet sobs escaped, and the eyes of my heart opened wide as Elsa created a magical winter wonderland experience for Anna. By the end of the "Do You Want To Build A Snowman?" montage, enough tears had flowed to thaw the edges of my frozen heart.

Somewhere in my spirit, I sensed a voice whispering, "This movie is a gift to you, Andrea. Receive it." So for the next two hours, my heart opened, and I wept as I watched my life unfold before my eyes in a beautiful metaphor on the screen.

SECTION ONE:
FORMING THE IDEAL ME

. . . .

CHAPTER 1

. . . .

Watching *Frozen* reminded me that I wasn't always so cold and cynical. The movie awakened my childlike aspiration for freedom to express my internal world with passionate creativity. As a young, empathetic girl, I had desperately wanted to connect deeply with others and have an extraordinary impact. But it seemed that the only way to secure those things was to gain and maintain respect from others. I was sure I could accomplish that goal by being the "best me" I could be.

So I'd set out to be good, strong and competent. Little did I know that my determination to earn respect for those qualities would become the very thing that drove a wedge between me and the meaningful relationships I so desperately craved.

As the years went by, the ideal self I constructed was mercifully dismantled in phases, and, bit by bit, the realization dawned that in protecting my image, I had paralyzed my ability to release the beautiful power I had to offer the world.

The day I saw the movie, I was still harboring pain and bitterness. My heart was still frozen, but I felt less alone as I watched Elsa struggle to reconcile the power inside of her with the needs of the people around her. That day I began to believe that Elsa wasn't the only one who needed to "let it go."

We called ourselves the "Von Moomey Family Singers" when no one was around. My younger sister and I had watched our parents sing in church all of our lives, and by the time we were five and seven, we followed in our parents' footsteps right up the stairs and onto the stage at church. It wasn't long before our musical numbers turned into family singing programs for nearby churches. Daniele and I sang the melody, Mom sang harmony, and Dad supported us underneath with the bass line.

We rolled up to churches in the area, pulling a little blue trailer filled with sound equipment to amplify our voices. Dad's job was to set everything up and be sure the amplifiers didn't get in the way of the true sound of our voices.

The message was Mom's job, and she took it seriously. She prepared notes with thoughts to be shared between songs. They were sincere and serious words, designed to set up each song so the people in the audience could feel every word.

Mom reminded us of our mission, "Don't forget, we are here to glorify God with our program. You never know who might be hurting today and needs to hear our message."

Our songs carried truth that resonated within us as we sang. Everything within me believed that when Jesus put a song in my heart, I needed to sing it.

It all felt very official. Church after small town church welcomed us as though we were there to give them a big gift. I loved being up on stage, but I wasn't sure it was OK to love performing as much as I did. We sang for God's glory, not our own. But that didn't stop people from complimenting us after performances. I wasn't sure what to do with the praise. Saying "thank you" made it feel like the whole thing was about me and how well I did. I wished I could sing my heart out and then go hide, but Mom and Dad insisted I learn to accept compliments graciously.

One comment I repeatedly received only confused me more. It seemed as though the same kind of elderly ladies cornered me after every concert. "You have a beautiful voice, dear! Always use it for God."

"Thanks. I will," I answered. I thought it was such an odd admonition.

They wouldn't say that if they knew me. Of course I will always use my voice for God.

Our family loved offering our performance as a gift to others. However, the wise reminders to use my voice for God raised a concern in me that perhaps my intense desire to perform wasn't good. I wanted to share the song in my heart, but I didn't want anyone to believe I was doing it for the wrong reasons. If they thought I was looking for applause, they wouldn't respect me. They wouldn't listen to me and truly consider what I was saying.

As an observant little girl with an insatiable curiosity to understand myself and other people, I had a lot of questions and believed that if I searched and thought hard enough, I could find the answers. And if I could just find the answers, I would be able to help everyone get along and use their voice for God, too.

Since I was seeking understanding all of the time, I believed I could achieve it. It was important to me to offer my perspective to every situation I found meaningful. It was like Jesus put a song of wisdom in my heart that needed to be sung.

But it wasn't long before I realized that not everyone wanted my "wisdom." Especially my little sister.

Daniele and I found that the best way to play together was to create dance routines in our basement. We twirled and swung and gyrated around our plastic-tiled basement floor with reckless abandon. We were young and free and expressive. The music tapped into our hearts and released dance moves we wouldn't dare show anyone else.

There was something about our sibling bond that allowed us to explore and release ourselves in unrestricted self-expression. But that bond came into question every time I tried to bestow my wisdom on her, like when I took voice lessons in third grade and attempted to share what I was learning.

"Daniele, if you take a little deeper breath, you'll be able to sing that note out longer," I offered my sister during a family rehearsal. She looked away and appeared to be ignoring my help.

I figured I just needed to explain it another way. "No, really, Daniele. It sounds OK, but if you breathe from your diaphragm, you'll be able to sing with a stronger voice."

Mom could tell our emotions were escalating, "She's fine, Andrea. Let it go."

"Yeah! Just leave me alone! You always try to correct me!" Daniele nearly yelled and then left the room.

It wasn't the first time I'd tried to help my sister and ended up hurting her. Nor was it the last.

In spite of my good intentions, it seemed my sister - and most females, for that matter - ended up getting upset when I tried to correct them. Dad didn't seem to mind so much. Maybe he understood me.

The emotional connection I shared with my mom and sister was powerful, but I measured my mind against my dad's. I watched him make decisions to lead our family with confident precision. And from what I could tell, most of the time the outcome was just what he intended. I wanted to move in the world like that. I wanted to awe and lead others with the confident precision of my mind, just like my dad.

It all made me wonder if I were different than other girls. They seemed to be more emotional than boys. I noticed that when girls giggled or made a big deal about how they looked, boys rolled their eyes. A strong need for boys' respect meant I was determined not to be the dramatic girl who was written off for being emotional. So I figured I just needed to hold back my feelings around boys.

Though just as emotional as other girls, I was quite calculating in the expression of that emotion. It was evident to me that boys had the power to determine if what I thought and said, mattered. Girls couldn't validate me like boys could. If I was to be heard, I needed boys to respect me.

The combination of deep thinking and intense feeling made it difficult for me to express those things and then connect with people who could relate to me on both levels at the same time. So when I failed to express myself appropriately, I turned inward and upward. Up to the playground swing.

The swing was my childhood "happy place." I loved feeling the exhilaration of defying the gravitational pull. On the swing, I could be in my own little world, taking in all of the action below and processing it deeply while still playing with my friends.

When I was on the swing, I could contemplate God and what it meant to be loved by Him. *I bet He will be happy with me if I throw a party for my teacher.*

I could plan out how I would handle difficult conversations. *If I let her know that I know she's having a party, maybe she'll invite me.*

And I could meticulously plan my vulnerability. *Would it give me away if I wrote, "Let's ride bikes together sometime" on his valentine?*

These were the kinds of conversations I wanted to have with a friend, yet many of my early elementary school nights were spent burying my heart in my pillow. I longed for a friend who wanted to share what they were thinking and feeling. But it is hard to find someone willing and aware enough to care about the confusing places in your heart as an adult, let alone as a child. No matter how often I connected with others, it was never enough. So I soaked in every meaningful moment with friends that I could, and then I went to the swing to share my mind and heart with God.

As I grew, I believed that God "got" me. He understood my thoughts and feelings, and He didn't seem to mind me going on and on about it. I could count on God to be curious about my heart, even when no one else seemed to be. We were pals.

I lived in the confident joy of knowing that whether anyone else understood me or not, God did. I loved feeling closer to him than anyone else. Our connection strengthened as I became more comfortable talking to Him. God and I were a team, and, deep down, I was convinced the song in my heart was gathering strength. I just wasn't sure if I should sing it.

CHAPTER 2

When a three-year-old finds a new way to do things, it's cute. When an eight-year-old questions her parents' plan, it's annoying. When a twelve-year-old finds loopholes in every directive, it's flat-out disrespectful. I was that kid with my parents.

As much as it must have annoyed her at times, I inherited my creativity from my mom. She always had fun ideas. She could tease and play make-believe with the silliest preschooler. Her dramatic renditions of storybooks delighted and transported us to worlds we could only imagine. Whether stenciling our favorite characters as a border on our bedroom walls or throwing elaborate parties for our birthdays, Mom always used her creativity to make people feel special. I wanted to make people feel like that too. And I certainly tried.

However, my creativity took on the form of determined innovation. When I felt motivated by love, it was a special power that could bring good things to the people around me. But when I felt threatened in any way, I replaced my determined innovation with negative counterparts. Creativity looked more like rebellion. Innovation felt more like rejection. And my determination made me stubborn.

I didn't want to appear rebellious, rejecting or stubborn, so I did my best to control my voice when it started to take on those qualities, at least with people outside of my family. I tried to cover up how I felt because I didn't want to be bad. I didn't want to be annoying or disrespectful, but it was hard to discern when it was OK to be innovative and determined and when it wasn't. I thought it would be best to push away these aspects about myself, but I couldn't. I wanted to be good, but I was highly aware of my impulse to let those bad and annoying things about me come out.

Any time a little weakness, rebellion or incompetence showed through, my desire to control what others thought of me took over. I totally denied the parts I didn't like and stuffed them back down. It got me in trouble - like the time I was the catcher for my junior high softball team....

"AHHHH!" I shouted in protest. The pitch was perfect. I hadn't moved my glove an iota to catch that softball. How could the umpire call it a ball?!

"If you complain about a call again, I'll throw you out of the game," he said.

"Oh – I'm not complaining! It just hurt!" I lied. I flat-out lied. I knew lying was wrong, but getting caught for having a bad attitude was worse.

"Right," He murmured sarcastically.

Pull it together, Andrea. Don't do that EVER again.

I didn't apologize. I just denied my wrongdoing. I didn't want to see that umpire ever again. The scene played over and over in my mind for years to come. It was one of the first times I was caught being blatantly rude and wrong. And I did not like being wrong.

In fact, I was pretty sure I was right about a lot of stuff because I spent so much time thinking everything through. Being right was such a large piece of my perceived identity that there was no room for doubt. It was easier to be sure, than to doubt. It was cleaner. It was simpler.

Being right just felt good. I was confident that if I could figure out God's ways, I would be important to God because I believed God highly valued people who's views and actions were ideal. Being the authority on a certain subject was satisfying. When I was right, it was important to me, and – I assumed – to God, that I communicate my correct thought to anyone who was wrong. It was my mission – my goal, purpose and duty.

If I were right, either people agreed so that I was respected even more, or they disagreed so I could explain my opinion even more. And I loved a good debate. Winning others over to my side was exhilarating. After all, that made me not only right, but also persuasive. I loved convincing others to believe I was right! But if I couldn't persuade them, I often wrote them off or shut them down with the authority of God Himself: "You're wrong." It was dangerously addictive territory.

Reconciling my desire to be right with my desire to connect with others was complicated. I didn't want to be or appear to be self-righteous, but I didn't want to compromise my voice, either. Eventually I found a way to utilize my perceived wisdom in the context of friendship. I realized that my desire for others to be curious about the hidden places in me was also a desire to draw out the hidden places in others. I could do for others what I wished they would do for me. And when people realized I was truly interested in them, they were open to my advice.

Thank God for junior high romance! I became, or certainly imagined myself to be, the wise "love doctor" to my group of friends. When she found out why I was tying up the phone line for so long every night, my mom laughed and called me "Dear Annie." I loved playing that role!

"Jeff, if you want her to notice you, you've got to think about what she likes, not just what you like."

"I'm sorry he broke up with you, Leslie, but I really don't think he was good for you in the first place. What kind of man do you want to marry? Someone who makes fun of people all the time or someone you can rely on?"

One Friday night, I went with friends to the movie theater to see Disney's live-action *Hook*. In the middle of the movie, I became highly aware of my position. Four couples surrounded me, one on the left, the right, in front and behind me. I, on the other hand, was accompanied by the strange combination of my analytical thoughts and intense emotion. There I was, surrounded by people, yet alone.

Well, it's You and me, Jesus. If this was the price I had to pay in the moment for being right all of the time, it was a burden I would have to bear. I had a long-term goal that would surely outlast any adolescent romance, so I might as well enjoy the show.

But the truth was, I wanted to be noticed too. One day I admitted my longing to a friend, "I'm here for everyone else, but I want someone to be interested in me too. It's silly to go out with people in junior high, but I still wish someone wanted me like that."

"I wouldn't worry about it, Andrea. You're the kind of girl who will probably end up marrying the first guy you date," she comforted.

Hmm…that wouldn't be so bad. I'll just get it right from the start.

"Is she supposed to sing that loud?"

The world came to a screeching halt as all eyes turned on me, and I turned beet red. My worst middle school fears were coming true in the middle of the music room. My voice was too loud.

Our teacher disagreed with her, and we moved on. However, I took note: *Don't stand out, or someone might call you out, Andrea.*

As tempting as it was sing more quietly or hold back my opinions to keep from standing out, I couldn't do it. My internal experience was so powerful that I found holding back my voice arduous.

My expressions were quite dramatic. When I was younger, I loved singing songs and reenacting plays in front of a mirror. I loved the drama! And I seemed to entertain others as well. But a little girl who communicated exuberantly in one way was sure to be expressive in others. My ability to delight people and show great compassion was countered by the reality that I could also convey intense fear and anger.

So I honed little tricks to keep myself under control. When I heard something that might make me cry and appear weak, I bit my tongue or turned away. Anger was reasoned away by belittling the other person in my mind. I pretended to have something in my eye when I cried during a movie. However, my attempts to filter or control the expression of my emotions weren't always successful. Sometimes those weak or dangerous, unwelcome feelings slipped out, and I wanted to hide.

My commitment to covering up or changing my unwanted feelings was so complete that I didn't realize I was hiding the real me. I totally thought I was being real. Really good. Really strong. Really competent. The real Andrea I believed I could and needed to be.

With all of my internal maneuvering, I was unaware that I was projecting a false image. My intention was simply to be the best version of myself. Authenticity and self-expression were so important to me that I was convinced that my facade was the real me. Entrenched in the good, strong and competent Andrea persona, I - and probably everyone else - believed that's who I was, even if it was nauseating.

This strengthened my belief that I could become whatever I imagined God wanted me to be. Whenever I heard my Sunday School teachers, pastors and parents declare what God wanted from me, I took note. I underlined and memorized and studied the Bible, particularly the letters in the New Testament that talked about how to live for God.

Desiring to be the best "Christian Andrea" I could be, I really believed I could achieve it. After all, I loved God and was determined to please Him. I wanted to be right with God and *right,* in general.

But that wasn't all. Since my early days on the swing, I longed to be close to God. Eager to be *closer* to God than I perceived others to be, I wanted my voice to stand out in God's ear, to be near to His side and to make a big difference in the world for Him. I was convinced that if I lived as the Bible said to live, if I had faith and didn't doubt, and if I believed all of the right things, I would secure my position as His right-hand girl.

My experience convinced me that the approval and respect of others was an indication of God's favor on me. So when images of men writing off emotionally-charged women played over and over in my mind, it motivated my desire to control my emotions with my logic.

Good. Strong. Competent. That was the ideal Andrea, the one whose voice rings with truth and power that God will use to change the world.

Deep down, I hoped that maybe I wasn't simply different, maybe my voice could actually be special. And I knew just how to find out.

CHAPTER 3

By my junior year of high school, I'd participated in honor choirs and performed solos for all sorts of concerts. My middle school goal of reading through the Bible was almost complete. Having worked hard to stand out for my faith, my convictions were known by my peers, and, for the most part, they didn't seem to mind.

Although connected and respected, I still felt different. At this point, I was ready to stretch my wings a little and see if I could land on a bigger stage and make a bigger impact with God. I was ready to find out if my voice really were special.

Since childhood, I had dreamed about singing the biggest solo in The Continentals, a Christian singing group for young adults. I secured the proper letters of recommendation, created my audition tape and got the approval of my parents.

Mom wasn't so sure about sending me off on my own for six weeks, but Dad was all for it. He loved to see his girls shine. I left nothing to chance. My essay was packed full of Bible verses and the passion of my heart to share Jesus with a hurting world. They accepted my application and a few weeks before the tour, a large manila envelope arrived in the mail.

"My music is here!" I ripped open the package and flipped through the songs until I came to a pastel pink piece of music entitled *Unbelievable Love.*

This is it, my heart pounded. *The biggest solo. My solo.*

The thought ran through my mind before I could stop it. God knew I wasn't in it for myself. Immediately, I covered my tracks.

"Lord, I want what You want for this experience. I want to sing this solo, but I know it may not be Your plan. Help me be open to Your will. Amen."

By the time I arrived in the Southern California rehearsal room for our group's training camp, I was prepared to audition for every solo and force myself to be content, whether I was chosen or not. I was there to serve, yet I still wondered if I had what it took to perform on this bigger stage. I didn't have to wait long to find out. Our director announced that after the break we would be auditioning for *Unbelievable Love.*

Here we go. Let's see what I can do.

When we came back from break, he asked who was interested. Glancing around the room, I was a bit apprehensive about competing with the other people who intended to audition for the song. They were all so friendly that I cringed at the idea of viewing them as rivals. Why did one of us have to get something the others wished they had? A two-tour veteran Continental went first. The other girl was blonde, bright, confident and had a beautiful voice. I rationalized that it would make sense if she got the biggest solo. She was, after all, three years older than I and seemed to know everyone, including the director. But she didn't get the solo. I got it.

I got the biggest solo in The Continentals tour. I got it!

The other kids in the group were kind. "You have a great voice!...You're the bomb!...Congratulations! You're going to rock that solo."

I wasn't so sure. Maybe the other girl should have received it. She was congratulatory to my face, but when she turned away, her eyes filled with tears. Past experiences flashed a big red warning sign in my mind: "You Hurt Her...You Hurt Her...You Hurt Her!" Discomfort gnawed at me. She had probably dreamed for weeks about singing this song on stage, just like I had.

Maybe I should have tried out for one of the quieter solos.

I shared my concerns with a couple of my new friends. They encouraged me to accept the director's decision. If I had prayed for God's will, I needed to accept it. The other girl would be fine.

I hoped so. As much as I wanted to prove that I was worthy of respect, I didn't like it when others got hurt along the way. I just wanted to sing my heart out, so why did singing my heart out always feel so crummy?

Despite the guilt I held for getting the biggest solo, I continued to long for additional affirmation. Without realizing what was happening, I sought out the best guy just like I sought out the biggest song. It wasn't that I was looking for a boyfriend, but I subconsciously wondered if I could impress someone on this bigger stage. Everyone was important to me, but something in me longed to hear I was special from the person I respected the most, in whatever setting I was in. For some reason, that person was always male.

It didn't take long for me to identify the person I needed to impress. John wore glasses as big as his smile and khaki corduroy pants in the summer, which proved both his sincere kindness and that he cared less about appearances than I did. He had a great voice and, most importantly, talked about God like he was close to Him. Perfect.

Everyone wanted John's attention, so I held back at first, because I knew that's what good girls did. They waited quietly for the best guys to notice them.

Sparks flickered between us from our first conversation. The electricity was intriguing, but I knew it couldn't go anywhere. There was a rule against romance on tour. We were here for God, not to let hormones run wild. I had no intention of breaking the rules, which made my drive to impress the best guy on tour even more tricky, but no less necessary. I didn't need to be romantically connected to him, just respected by him. I just wanted to know if I were special.

There's nothing quite as dramatic as a group of adolescent performers on a tour bus for hours on end. The percentage of expressive people compared to quiet people was flipped from real life in our group. Melodramatic voice and body gestures were the rule, not the exception. I could let my hair down, my face contort and my hands fly. Seat partners chosen at each stop sat with one ear bud in each person's ear as we created goofy choreography to songs as we silently mimicked them.

We grew to care deeply for each other and entered into serious conversations quite often. Those meaningful discussions were my playground. I owned this territory. My heart-to-heart conversations had matured since my days as the junior high love doctor. If I sensed one of my friends was hurting, I found my way to her side and searched deep in her eyes for the pain. My heart touched her hurting heart in conversation, and something magical happened: We felt connected. She felt loved, and I felt important. An important helper to God, that is. But when I connected with the most respected guy, whoever he was, I felt even closer to God.

One day I grabbed for my stuff in the overhead bin and found an envelope. My hands shook a little as I stuffed it into my bag and walked off the bus. What did the most respected guy on tour have to say to me in a note that he couldn't say in person? I ducked into the bathroom and unwrapped John's words, written just for me.

I don't think you understand how much your friendship has meant to me. I do have many male friends who are really strong Christians, but it is rare for me to be in the presence of a woman who has as strong a faith and as caring and gentle heart as I found within you.

I swallowed hard and attempted to change into my costume for the show. I knew I was going to sing the top out of my biggest solo that night because I'd done it – I'd impressed the most respected guy there. Worship seemed to overflow from my heart, but perhaps it was the thrill of validation.

I really am special! God sees me. He gets me. And He likes me. I know, because John does.

After singing in churches in the southwestern United States for a few weeks, we boarded a 747 and headed to England. You would have thought we were the first generation to cross the pond after the Boston Tea Party. Our group of brash teenagers hit the streets of London sporting American flag paraphernalia, full of adventure and superior rebel spirit. John and I seemed to manage to be in the same group of tourists wherever we went. Or perhaps I managed it, I wasn't sure. I was sure that no matter where we went, I would have more fun if he were around.

"You really need to break out of your box, Andrea," he told me once. His concern was sincere, yet gentle. How could he know me for three weeks and have a better idea of who I was deep down than anyone at home? Better than I knew myself?

"I'm not sure I know how to do that," I admitted. He seemed determined to be the one to show me.

Our week in England included a day at Cambridge, the town with the historic university. Dreams of being as smart and being taken as seriously as Cambridge students inspired me, despite the dreariness of the day. We unloaded and were instructed on how long we could wander the streets before it was time to get on the bus again. I found myself with John and a few other friends, peering into quaint little boutiques as we walked down the street. We walked right past another shop until I realized what was inside.

"Hats!" I turned on my heel and right into the little boutique. There were big hats with bows and black hats with white ribbon; delicate hats and big, bright, brilliant hats illuminated by soft lights lined the walls and filled the racks in the middle of the room. I stood in awed contemplation.

In spite of loving how I looked in hats, I had no intention of ever wearing one. Hats expected to be noticed. They sat on a head like a neon sign flashing, "Tell me I'm beautiful!" Good grief! I wasn't about to admit I wanted to hear that.

My lips betrayed me when I sighed, "I love hats!" My friends chuckled as John placed one on my head.

"What are you doing?!" Since I wouldn't be buying a hat, it seemed appropriate only to look and not touch. I didn't handle stern looks from clerks with any amount of grace, nor did I want to get in trouble.

"You're getting a hat!" he informed me.

Looking at the price tag, I did a little conversion in my head. "No, I'm not! I have no place to wear a hat. I can't spend $60 on a hat that I won't ever wear!"

John grinned and replaced the hat on my head with another one, "Yes, you can. You need to break out of your box." They continued to dress me with hats until they grabbed a little straw number with a pink flower fastened to the brim. When I glanced in the mirror, I stopped breathing. The girl staring back at me was a stranger. She wasn't practical, strong and right about everything. She was soft and beautiful. Her eyes weren't looking for respect. They were open, inviting me to enjoy her, just as she was.

John grabbed it off of my head and went to the clerk. "What are you doing?!" I asked incredulously, after snapping out of my trance.

"Getting you a hat," he stated.

I looked in terror at my other friends. What in the world would a practical, Midwestern girl do with a straw hat from Cambridge? "I'm not getting a hat," I pleaded with them.

"Yes, you are!" they laughed. Clearly, they didn't understand how insane, and what a big waste of money this was! But they went in on it with John and bought me the hat.

Words refused to form in my mouth when he handed me the bag. We started walking down the streets of Cambridge, when John stopped me and pulled the hat out of my bag, and placed it on my head. A smile escaped but I felt awkward and said as much. "This isn't me!" I insisted. And yet a tiny bit of me wished it were.

John stopped my protests with his serious glance and then smiled. "You look cute."

I wasn't about to put a hat on my own head, but John just did for me what I'd been waiting forever for someone to do. He insisted so I wouldn't have to admit my desire.

All resolve to not betray anyone's heart or break any rules evaporated right along with my insistence that I remain practical and boring. I didn't want to hurt anyone or get in trouble, but I didn't know who I was anymore. I followed my friends down to the river and into a little gondola-like boat. Six of us climbed in; I wished it were two. As the gentleman guiding us planted his pole on the riverbed and pushed us under an old stone bridge in a foggy haze, I drifted off into dreamland, and stayed there for months.

The last day of tour, John broke the rules and acknowledged the spark between us. I didn't want to cause any problems, but I rationalized that it was necessary. This wasn't just about John. I wasn't who I used to be; I was a beautiful girl who wears a hat.

For the first time since childhood, I allowed my heart to leap and dance and sing, unrestrained. I belonged with someone who adored me, and I was in awe of him. God was so good!

A couple visits, three months, a bunch of phone calls and dozens of letters later, I was still living in my fairytale, and every one of my friends and teachers knew it. I didn't care what anyone thought anymore. A great guy was enamored with me, and it felt incredible. How could two people be any happier? There was something about the hat that took my head out of the game No intrusion of logic was going to ruin my euphoria.

Mom was never pleased with my situation and let me know as much. Uncertain about how to help her see that this was clearly God's plan for me, I figured that she was simply blinded by her desire to have me go to college and raise a family in central Nebraska. She didn't understand that I'd found a bigger stage, and there was no going back now. No matter how strong the winds of opposition blew, I held my hat firmly in place.

Until one day he called. I went to the phone in our home office, settling in on the floor, a smile already anticipating the voice of his adoration. But he sounded different. The insider voice that characterized our interactions had become matter-of-fact.

"I was talking to a friend of mine here at college. She goes to a church like yours and said that there are a lot of differences between our churches. Since I'm going to be a pastor, I just don't think this is going to work."

"Oh. OK. I understand." There wasn't much to say. "So I guess you won't be coming here for your fall break."

"We should stay friends, Andrea," he offered.

I blinked away the agony of that thought. Determined not to lose his respect now, I decided to handle this with poise and speak in his matter-of-fact tone. "Of course. Talk to you later, John."

Steady, shallow breaths undergirded me as I hung up the phone. I opened the office door, and Mom saw me from her room.

"That was short. How is John?" She asked.

"He's fine. We broke up." I stated without emotion.

"Oh Andrea, I'm sorry. Are you OK?" I knew my mom felt bad for me, but I also knew she was relieved he wouldn't be taking me away from her. "I'm surprised you're not crying."

"I'm fine. I just...woke up from a dream."

Somehow my feet found their way down the stairs and into my bedroom. I could hardly move, but my hands had a job to do. I packed away every letter and took down every picture. There was no sense in making a bigger idiot of myself. Like a fool, for months I'd been swinging on the gates of my heart. I had no intention of admitting the shame I felt when I fell off. The only way I could save face was to snap back to reality. Back to good, strong, competent Andrea. I pulled my heart down from the clouds and secured it behind a fortress of logic.

I saw the straw hat with the little pink flower and then looked around the room. "This belongs in a box."

I won't make that mistake again. It was all just one big dream. I'm not the kind of girl who wears a hat.

CHAPTER 4

Every once in awhile, a memory or a glimpse of the hat caught me off-guard, and, for a brief moment, my heart levitated as it had for those few months I was with John. As soon as I realized what was going on, I grabbed it and stuffed it back down into my chest. I had to stay grounded.

You can't have feelings for someone you aren't going to marry, Andrea.

Nearly a year later, it was time for me to head to college. Having packed a new book, I read it on the way to Belmont University in Nashville. It offered the perfect remedy to the humiliation I experienced when I returned from dreamland and reentered the real world. I determined to take the advice of this author who appeared to know exactly what God thought of relationships. I, too, would guard my heart and "kiss dating goodbye." Why give a piece of it away to a guy if I weren't sure I would marry him? I wasn't sure how many pieces were left.

The idea of guarding my heart gave me permission to close off the possibility of exposing it to rejection again. I certainly wouldn't want to have feelings for someone who wasn't sure to be my husband someday! I wasn't foolish. And what would that say about my relationship with God? If I were close to God, He would direct me in His ways so I would be blessed and not have to deal with the pain of a broken heart.

I convinced myself that I didn't have to make that mistake again.

My interpretation of "guard your heart" perpetuated the notion that if I allowed myself to get hurt, I was weak. And weak was shameful. Images of giggling girls with crushes circulated in my mind. Reminders of emotionally-charged women being written off, unseen and unheard pierced my heart. I wasn't about to let that happen to me. It made sense that I ought to focus on my relationship with God, and then, when the right man came along, we could keep emotions out of it until we knew we were the right fit. No risk. No humiliation. I could get back to being the good, strong and always-right Andrea I believed I could be.

My mom, dad and sister helped me load a few treasured items into the back of our minivan, and then I tucked myself into the back seat with my book and patched up heart. I had to prepare myself because my friend John suggested we stop and visit on our way. Hours later, we pulled into a café. I sat stuck in a circular booth with John and my family for a whole hour of agonizing chitchat. When we finally headed out to the car, John cornered me.

"How are you, really?" His caring eyes peered into mine as if he were looking for a sign of the girl he once knew. I wasn't about to be sucked into his empathetic trap. I looked him straight in the eye, without an ounce of feeling, and said, "I'm good. I'm reading a book right now. I think it might be good for you to read." He was already dating someone else.

After hearing the title and premise of the book, he turned toward me with a furrowed brow. "Are you sure this is good for you? I'm worried about you."

Oh, brother. Why is he so concerned? It's not like living in dreamland was a good idea. I basically gave him a piece of my heart. I just want to take it back and have him leave me alone. He doesn't get me. Apparently he was right. We believe different things about God.

"I'm fine. Have a good year at college, John." I smiled and joined my family in the van.

I didn't see him again. I made my way through my college years staying true to my determination to kiss dating goodbye. Of course, my radar set was always set to find the most respected guy in every campus ministry I attended so I could impress him. And, of course, I secretly dreamed that "he" would notice me and think I was the girl he respected most. But I never moved beyond hope. There was no way I would let that guy know that I admired him. There was no way I would be caught longing for someone God didn't plan to give me.

I even made it a practice to keep my hopes about specific guys out of my journal. What if someone read it someday? I didn't want to be humiliated again. Girls who are close to God don't give pieces of their hearts away to even the most respected guys. The girls close to God don't even hope to do it, because those girls listen to God and wait for His best.

So I subconsciously determined to wait for the guys I respected most to tell me what God had to say. But apparently He wasn't telling any of them to move toward me.

The problem with refusing to admit a crush or show my weaknesses was that shame grew wild in my secret's fertile soil and cultivated deeply rooted doubts. Doubts grew long tendrils of anxiety, and anxiety crowded and choked out what otherwise would have been healthy relational interactions.

I have to be strong.
I must keep it together.
I can't let him know.
I am not OK!
What is wrong with me?!

Oh, nothing. Nothing is wrong, because I can be the ideal Andrea I dream of being. I mean, I can do all things through Christ who gives me strength, right? I can be strong. I can be good. I can be competent. So I will.

Being strong all the time required serious strategy, so it was a good thing I excelled in strategizing. I figured that since my face always betrayed what I felt, I had to get really good at convincing myself I didn't feel unwanted feelings.

While at college, I didn't allow the intensity of my longing, fear or sadness to reach beyond what I could control. I certainly didn't want to feel desire. If I flirted too much or appeared too needy around certain people, I backed away from them. If I felt scared, I would square my shoulders and walk right into the situation. If I were sad, I would find someone or something to blame and feel indignant about since self-righteous anger made me feel powerful.

Power was absolutely necessary because, above all things, I needed to guard my heart. I didn't have any intention of getting hurt again.

After a few months, I went to a book study with one of my college friends in Nashville. The only reason I wanted to go was to be around grownups where we could have good discussion. Maybe one of them would take a special interest in me. Maybe I would find a mentor. I really wasn't all that interested in reading a book, though the title *Connecting* intrigued me. It took a while for me to get into it, but once I did, I began to resonate deeply with the author.

"It's like this guy is in my head!" I told a friend. I had never experienced such a correlation of ideas with another person before. He seemed to be explaining me:

> *...[S]omething is poured out of one and into the other that has the power to heal the soul of its deepest wounds and restore it to health. The one who receives experiences the joy of being healed. The one who gives knows the even greater joy of being*

used to heal. Something good is in the heart of each of God's children that is more powerful than everything bad. It's there, waiting to be released, to work its magic. But it rarely happens.[1]

His words described what I'd been experiencing for years: connecting "magic." Something life-giving happened when I cared about friends and they shared what was on their hearts. I just wished someone would take that kind of interest in me too. Not just anyone, someone special.

But it wasn't happening quite like I'd imagined it. I felt like I was looking at the world through a pane of glass. God and I were on one side, and everyone else was on the other. Guarding my heart seemed to be keeping me close to God but far away from others. I wasn't sure what I was doing wrong, but I knew that, above all else, I had to keep protecting my heart. I left that book study without a special connection with one of the older women, yet I left believing I'd found a mentor.

After reading *Connecting,* I picked up another book by Dr. Larry Crabb. *Shattered Dreams* introduced me to the idea of self-protection, the means by which we guard our hearts from the threat of pain. In that book he shared a vision for how emotional pain could help us detach from the fake parts of ourselves so we could find our true selves. The more I thought about it, the more I realized that my true self wanted to be found.

> *Happy people, though they're right to be happy, face a subtle danger...They can easily slip into a concern for the less fortunate that carries with it a mood of judgment: If they were more like me, they would be given the blessings I have...Unhappy folks face their own unique temptation. Publicly they tell the more fortunate how glad they are for all who are so blessed; privately they wish that the happy person's path would hit a ditch.*[2]

Without realizing it before that point, my concern for others had carried with it a mood of judgment. I'd been constantly searching for the right way to live, God's best. If I did things God's way, He would give me a wink and a nod, and I could walk through life happy and confident, knowing that I was right. Then I could sing the song in my heart.

My friends and family would also be happy, and we would feel blessed.

But Larry Crabb was saying that I was looking for the wrong thing. I could hardly believe it!

> *Happy people do not love well. Joyful people do...Happy people rarely look for joy. They're quite content with what they have. The foundation of their life becomes the blessings they enjoy. Although they may genuinely care about those less fortunate and do great things to help, their central concern is to keep what they have. They haven't been freed to pursue a greater dream. That's why they cannot love well. In His severe mercy, God takes away the good to create an appetite for the better, and then, eventually, He satisfies the new appetite, liberating them to love.*[3]

God has a greater dream for me to dream? It occurred to me that avoiding pain and attempting to maintain the level of influence I had wasn't getting me very far. After reading the book, I realized I didn't have to live to guard my heart from pain and heartache. I could live to love others, despite the pain and heartache. The vision that I could be released from the pressure to protect myself called to me. I had always wanted to strive to be the best Christian I could be, but working to become the ideal version of myself had left me dissatisfied. Reading *Shattered Dreams* stirred my desire to dig into a deeper level of intimacy with God and others. So I prayed, *"God, in your mercy, break me. I don't just want to be happy. I want deep joy."*

....

CHAPTER 5

....

In 2001, I was a senior music education major at the University of Nebraska-Kearney, having transferred there two years earlier. I'd spent the past few years exploring performance, teaching and relationships, and my struggle to understand it all culminated one April night.

At the end of the school year I found myself driving home from the last rehearsal of Karisma, a little gospel choir I'd started that year as a ministry. My goal had been to give other students the opportunity to sing their hearts out just as I had when I was in a gospel choir in Nashville. Also I was itching to see if I had the chops to conduct with passion and lead with wisdom. Our little group of 25 college students rehearsed in a church and performed a few times that semester. We even organized a campus ministry rally where we performed. For the most part, we enjoyed it.

But that night I wondered, what difference I had really made with the choir? It seemed that no matter how inspiring I attempted to be, they were still holding back their voices to some degree and looking at me funny as I waved my hands in front of them.

Had I done the right thing by starting Karisma? Was I pushing myself and my agenda on others by acting on my own desires? Was I creating opportunities for others, or was I creating opportunities for myself?

Was it OK for me to produce great ideas and motivate groups of people to act on them?

When I try to make difference, I feel pushy. But when I don't, I feel like a pushover. I'm completely frustrated either way!

I felt lost in my reflections. It was time for me to become a music teacher, then build a family and life I loved, but I was nowhere close to knowing what that should look like for me.

Besides, I hadn't dated anyone for five years. I wasn't sure why, but it seemed some older women at church sure did. When they realized I wasn't dating, they would say, "You must not be ready yet."

Barf.

Locking my car, I headed up to my apartment. I was done with the gospel choir. Done with music education classes and campus ministries. Above all, I was done holding out hope that God would help me find my husband at college.

Flicking on the lights, I went straight to my room. Items of memorabilia from high school and college surrounded me. Uncomfortable with the idea of tossing them into a box without honoring them, drawer-by-drawer, I picked up old papers, letters and pictures. For brief moments at a time, I held each memory in my heart with a smile and a tear before packing it away.

My hand thoughtlessly grabbed an old high school senior picture, and I glanced at the straw hat on my head. In an instant, my heart flipped over, and I became the cute girl on the gondola, wearing the straw hat from Cambridge. Longing unfurled in my stomach and made it to my throat, where it begged to come out as a sob. I blinked and swallowed and shook the feeling back down.

Whew! That was close.

I came back to the floor of my bedroom, my back pressed up against the bed and my head bare as ever. *What just happened?*

My reflective mood wouldn't allow the moment to pass without scrutiny. It didn't make sense. I had to face the fact that the thought of John still made my heart flip over.

John and I broke up five years ago, and I haven't been in contact with him since I went to college. How could I possibly still have feelings for him?

I recalled the admonition I'd embraced four years before, not to hand out pieces of my heart. But every once in a while, I would be caught off guard with a thought about the time in my life when I felt beautiful. And every time, I responded with a blink and a swallow and a shake of my head.

I'd been doing this for years! Was that it? Had I given him a piece of my heart that I could never get back?

This isn't OK. I think I want to find a husband, but how can I find someone new when I continue to have such powerful feelings for an old flame? I figured that denial would have extinguished it by now. I'm done with this, too.

"God, what should I do?"

If hiding from my feelings and shoving them back down inside of me hadn't worked for five years, maybe I needed to face them head-on. The words of Dr. Larry Crabb entered my mind and I realized that this dream had already shattered. I just needed to acknowledge it.

Reaching into the back of my closet, I pulled out an old box with a picture album and dozens of handwritten letters. I rummaged through the bottom of the box until I found it. With trembling hands, I loaded the cassette tape into my player.

"Dear God, help me."

I wept as songs carefully curated for me by John five years before filled the room. One by one, I opened up and read the letters he wrote to me and grieved. Then, one by one, I put them away and prayed.

What is it that makes me so sad? If he wasn't the man for me, why does it hurt so much? What do I miss if it's not him? It can't be him. What feeling is deeper than missing him?

That's it! It's the FEELING!

It was a feeling that I missed, the feeling that I was worth the letters, the songs and the hat. I sought him out back then like I sought out the biggest solo, to see what I was capable of. My feelings were real, but holding onto them wasn't worthwhile. John wasn't the object of my desire anymore. The feeling that I belonged with someone was. He was the guy on tour I most respected, so when he told me I was something special, I believed him. He made me happy because he made me feel good about myself.

If it's simply a feeling that I miss and not those particular circumstances, then I am free! It doesn't have to be John. Someday someone else will come along and connect with me like that.

From that moment on, my heightened emotional response was no longer tied to a person. There was no need to feel embarrassed. No need to hide from my feelings. The good grief I experienced that night in my room released me from the pressured shame I'd allowed to lock me up inside. It helped me let go of something that was good and gave me an appetite for something better, convincing me that embracing my brokenness was the path to connection.

It didn't occur to me at the time, but maybe it was the path to having an impact too.

SECTION TWO:
FINDING THE REAL ME

CHAPTER 6

A year later I was living with my parents and teaching K-12 band and vocal music at a school in a small nearby town. However, the position didn't seem to fit well, and my mind continued to pester me in quiet moments.

I wished I could get paid to think of questions. That was a job I could handle. No longer under the illusion that I would find all the answers, I just needed to ask the questions. But my introspective processing was driving me crazy and sometimes seemed to do the same to those around me.

Why in the world did God make me like this? There are perfectly good Christian people out there who aren't plagued by the intensity of thoughts and feelings I have inside.

The worst part was that my verbal personality meant I couldn't keep it to myself. My intense curiosity spilled out onto the people around me. I knew it drove some folks nuts, but what in the world was I supposed to do about it?

"Lord, please give me peace. For some crazy reason You have given me a brain that likes to sort things out. I pray that You would be my source of wisdom. Please bring these thoughts to some kind of focus that

will edify people and glorify You. There must be purpose for all of this. Help me find it. Don't let me waste what You've given me."

Theological questions I'd been wrestling with since my high school youth group days still wouldn't go away. Searching for answers seemed to be the only way I could understand my identity and role in life. I constantly struggled to find an inner peace that would allow me to feel OK about God, who I was, and how I was supposed to interact in the world.

I wasn't sure how I would ever pay for it, but I knew I had to settle my mind and heart before I could find a way to express it to the world. So I took off to Trinity Evangelical Divinity School near Chicago.

When I walked into my seminary dorm room the next fall, all of the hope I had placed in the experience sank to my feet. The room had a twin bed, dresser, desk, and a small, cut-out closet with no doors. The walls were a dirty white, and the room was the size of a large bathroom. The walls seemed to close in on me and my 24-year-old self.

Shouldn't I have a real job by now and live in a real apartment with space to breathe?! No sooner had that thought passed when there was a knock on my door.

"Hello!" Standing in the hall was a boisterous woman with blonde hair as thick as her Australian accent. Marion introduced herself and welcomed me to the dorm. She filled the space around her with a robust intellect and a compassion only tempered by her fierce passion for justice. No wonder – she was a lawyer who gave up her campus ministry in England to pursue her Master of Divinity degree.

Wow. This woman gets around! Maybe this will be an amazing experience after all.

I immediately identified Marion as someone I could look up to. She was seven years older than I was and certainly had a lot more real world experience than I did. Marion was, in many ways, what I'd always wanted to be. She had a strong voice with a quick tongue, and she wasn't afraid to use it. She made measuring ideas against Scripture seem liberating. And her concern for and interest in the students and faculty at seminary outdid my own.

As we became better acquainted, I realized Marion showed her heart in her face. The sparkles in her eyes always gave her away. Whatever form they took, it was an intense one. They flashed hot when she stood against threats of injustice. When others shared their pain, the sparkles softened and comforted the soul of the one with her. And when Marion felt her own pain, her eyes washed with tears and then turned back to caring passionately about others once more.

I admired Marion. I'd never met anyone like her, and I was convinced God put her in my path to help shape me. Could it be that I found someone more passionate than myself? She amazed me.

It didn't take long before I realized that I was one of the more social people on campus. Apparently people trained to be pastors and missionaries were not all that concerned about their social lives. I, on the other hand, was immensely curious about those around me. When I realized how serious they all were, I felt it was my duty to draw them out and see them for who they truly were.

Every single person I met fascinated me. Perhaps it was the nature of graduate work, but everyone there seemed to have a song in their own heart, some kind of personal experience of transformation that drew them to this place. Some people were passionate about learning how to read the Bible. Some wanted to teach it. Others kept talking about how they were doing everything "for the sake of the Gospel."

I wondered where I fit in. I was certainly interested in learning about God and the Bible, but I wanted to understand people better. How would God have us interacting with each other? How does He move to heal and transform us? More than anything, I wanted to know what to do with myself. What does God think of women like me? What did He create me to do? The questions begged for answers and drove me in an intense pursuit of clarity.

The ambiguity of my purpose made choosing a degree program feel like gambling, something seminary students were not allowed to do. My normal course of action would have been to choose the most challenging option, but I had no idea how I would pay back a three-year Master of Divinity degree or where in the world I would use it. So I printed out the course schedule and circled every class I was particularly interested in taking. When I finished, I compared my interests with the degree offerings and settled in on the Masters in Counseling Ministry option.

I chuckled when I put my degree titles together. They aptly described someone with a plethora of interests, who couldn't make up her mind: music/education/counseling/ministry. Counseling Ministries wasn't a particularly marketable degree, but I wasn't sure any of them would be for a woman from my religious tradition. However, if I were only here to gain peace about the theological, relational and personal questions that plagued me, it would be worth it.

Because of the nature of my degree, my course load was lighter than most. At first I wondered if I were making the most of my opportunity. Was I squandering my time and money by having a lighter course load than I ever had in college? But as I witnessed the pressured stress that weighed other students down and kept them locked away in their rooms and the library, I gave thanks for the buffer in my time and energy. I also realized that in limiting my personal needs, I left room in my life to be available to the people around me.

Conversations were struck up with all manner of individuals that I ran into at class, in my dorm or the cafeteria. My genuine curiosity seemed to be a welcome balm for lonely seminary students and gave them the opportunity to remember their purpose, when translating Hebrew and Greek overwhelmed them.

"What brought you to seminary?"

"What are you wrestling with in class?"

"What is it like being a woman in the MDiv program?"

I asked all of the questions I wished other people would ask me. We were all stretching in our faith and grappling to understand God. Some of those struggles manifested in relational interactions among us. Some of them turned into insomnia and depression. But more often than not, the struggle was like iron sharpening iron as we were transformed into people who longed to see God heal the world as He was healing us.

I listened to the amazing souls around me, I kept hearing a phrase that had previously struck me as trite. After hearing their personal stories, however, I began to realize there was great depth implied when people said they were here "for the sake of the Gospel."

Maybe they say that with sincerity because the Gospel really did change them. I wish I had a better testimony.

I wasn't so foolish as to believe that I should have rebelled more in my youth or to wish for a painful childhood. However, the thought crossed my mind that the people had those kinds of experiences seemed to have more passion to share the Gospel than I had ever hoped to have.

The truth was, I was tired of hearing that Jesus died for my sins. I had asked Jesus into my heart when I was five and asked to be baptized when I was six. I'd always lived my life knowing that Jesus died for my sins so I could go to heaven. And yet, that knowledge bored me. I wanted to listen to sermons about how I should live my life and find answers about my identity. I wanted to help people in their relationships with one another.

Now, while watching my friends take communion, I considered the stories they'd told me about their past and how God had brought them out of it. I sensed a fresh depth of meaning in all of it.

Before I could stop the thoughts, I prayed: *"God, help me understand the Gospel. I want to know it like my friends do."* I never would have expected my relationships with men to lead me there.

CHAPTER 7

Once the semester got rolling, I called my grandma to let her know how much I was enjoying the opportunity to learn and grow in the seminary environment. The conversation went something like this:

"Well, that's nice. But make sure you don't talk too much in class, dear," Grandma cautioned.

"Why is that, Grandma?" I wondered.

"You don't want the boys to think you're smarter than they are. You've got to let them answer questions and let them win every once in awhile so they don't give up."

Was a girl with great passion supposed to tone it down all of the time so she doesn't intimidate men and end up alone? It was hard for me to imagine playing coy in class, but I still wondered if it were true. Could I be who I was without annoying or intimidating others and isolating myself? Was my creative introspection that bad? Was it really that bad to have a strong voice and express it passionately?

Our conversation made me think of a ministry situation I had been in with a young man a few months earlier. I had determined to hold back my thoughts and opinions about the way things should go and just offer them when he asked. My intention was to give him space to explore his own leadership abilities. The problem was that he never did ask. I was shocked to be in a position where I was expected to be a leader, yet I had no voice because I didn't assert it.

"I hate being a woman and I highly doubt I could ever handle being married. God, I know You don't make mistakes, but I am ticked because why would You give me these gifts and put me in a woman's body? If I were a man, this wouldn't be an issue. But I don't know what I'm supposed to do with myself – hold back or let go?"

How would men feel, I wondered, if they found out women were coddling them because they didn't believe men could handle their passion? How many women walked through life convinced if they lived into the fullness of who they are, that they would intimidate or annoy the people around them and end up alone?

The phone call with my grandma kept me asking God what He planned on doing with me. If I held back, I would feel like a doormat, and my gifts would be wasted. If I let my voice go, I would hurt people. They would feel intimidated or judged. I certainly didn't want that, so I insisted that there must be a better option.

I filled a 3 inch navy blue binder with articles, Scripture and quotes I found on the internet. Neon colors stained the pages in horizontal lines, and ink spilled my questions and reflections in the margins as I attempted to understand what God thought of me as a woman.

Should I suppress the inner drive to take initiative and lead? What is ministry supposed to look like for me? What am I ever supposed to do with myself?

At the heart of my questions was a deeper one. *Will I ever find a man with whom I belong? Will he love and respect the powerful aspects of my personality and gifting rather than be annoyed or threatened by them?*

I believed God was capable of creating a man that would be a good match for me, but I wasn't sure He liked me enough to do it. If I were "too much," it seemed the only action I could take was to find someone who was at least as much or more than me. Perhaps if I found a stronger leader, deeper thinker, and someone more passionate than I was, I wouldn't have to suppress my own leadership, depth and passion. The question was, did he exist?

Even in the married Christian leaders I knew, I saw few relationships to which I could relate. I wondered if God had made a mistake with me. Why did I have to possess such a burning drive to solve all of the problems in my mind? And what good would it do even if I did? If the gifts that I had only seemed to be valid and accepted when used by a man, why had God given them to me? Or was there actually a way for a woman to express the gifts that often were viewed as masculine?

Trying to figure out how I could fit into society and ministry frustrated me, but it occurred to me that perhaps it would become more clear when I got married. Maybe everyone else was right in believing that I wasn't good enough on my own. I heard a number of times that others were convinced I would end up a pastor's wife. Maybe I was created to be a partner in ministry. Maybe that would make sense of my identity.

Still, in the dark of night, I was convinced that I thought too deeply, felt too intensely and expressed it all too powerfully ever to belong or have an influential voice as a woman. I was ticked off and trembling at the same time. My consolation was that I knew I could let God know how I felt without being too much for Him. I knew God could handle me, even if men could not.

One evening in September, I felt inspired by the fact that reading and thinking was my job for the next two years. I grabbed my blanket and a book and went out to the grassy commons area. I breathed in the warm air, glancing at the stars beginning to peek through the sliver of sky above me. A sigh escaped as I settled into my new happy place.

Only a few minutes passed before someone strolled by. I offered a friendly "hi."

"What are you reading?" he asked. Shane was a second year student leader who took every new student under his wing. I looked up and smiled.

"It's called *The Safest Place on Earth,* by Larry Crabb."

"Oh, yeah. I've read a few of his books. I really appreciate his take on relationships. His thinking really took a turn a few years ago."

Have I actually found someone else here who thinks about the things I do? Someone who appreciates Larry Crabb like I do?!

Our conversation continued, delving into a number of relational topics and leadership. By the time he walked off, I was convinced he was going to have a huge impact on the Christian community. He didn't seem at all intimidated or annoyed by my passion for the subject. It was exciting to get to know someone like that.

Something spiritually important appeared to be going on inside of me as a result of our conversation. I read Psalm 139, and it made me weep. As many times as I'd heard those verses before, never had they brought out such emotion in me.

> *"You created me in my inmost most being; You knit me together in my mother's womb. I praise You because I am fearfully and wonderfully made; Your works are wonderful, I know that full well." (Psalm 139:13-14)* [4]

Simply meeting a man who understood my interest in relationships me made me hope that it was OK to be me. Maybe I didn't need to change my personality. God had made me with these gifts, this intellectual capacity, this heart and calling for a reason. Whether or not that reason included this man who exceeded my expectations didn't matter. I held on to hope that I could be who God had created me to be.

A few days later, Shane shared more of his story with me. He tried to give me the short version, but, like an expert interviewer, I kept asking him questions, and he kept opening up. I couldn't believe the pain he'd experienced. It made me wonder, why was I so blessed? Why do some people have to endure so much?

We were in the middle of our conversation when other people came over. I felt uncomfortable with the way the conversation ended. He had talked about the heavy details of his life for the better part of an hour, and I never got to tell him that I appreciated his opening up, nor did I get to speak any words of encouragement. I felt uncomfortable without those two things to close the conversation. I knew what it was like to share and have my heart go unacknowledged, and I certainly didn't want him to feel that way. So I determined to affirm him for his transparency.

With this simple intention, I left him a note since he wasn't in his room. However, he didn't know me well enough to understand my motive, so a while later he came to my window and asked to speak with me.

"Hey." He held up my little note.

I smiled. He must have appreciated it. "Hey."

"I just want to be sure there isn't any misunderstanding about why I shared with you."

"Oh?" I was surprised that he would say such a thing. "Well, I've had a lot of conversations with people where they share really personal stuff and when that happens, I want to honor that."

"OK." He was visibly relieved. "It just seems like girls think I like them all the time. It's really annoying. I'm glad we're good. Thanks!"

Well, it's good to have that cleared up! It's a blessing, really. Now I know for sure, and we don't have to worry about it.

The next couple weeks, I kept my distance from Shane. However, one night when I ran into him, I could tell that something was on his mind, so I inquired and he invited me to go on a walk. We ended up talking about the Christian brother/sister relationship and how to deal with the

49

confusion that naturally could come with it. He let me know that he had been thinking more about getting to know someone in particular, and he wondered what I thought he should do.

"My problem is that if I don't normally initiate interaction with friends, I have to go out of my way to get to know someone. And that messes with a girl's mind. I want to guard her heart because I feel it's my responsibility. So wouldn't it be better to flat out ask her out so she knows what I'm thinking?"

I tried with all my strength to keep my guard up. There I was, walking through a dark campus on a crisp autumn night with the man who made me feel like I wasn't a mistake. I tried not to let the thought surface, but it did anyway.

Could it be that he is talking to me in code? Did he realize in the past couple of weeks that he really is interested in me?

"Maybe you could change the way that you interact with friends so it won't be so unnatural to get to know her," I managed to suggest. He didn't think that was possible. "Well, ultimately you can't take full responsibility for guarding a woman's heart. She is responsible for it as well, and she will need to get over it if she gets disappointed."

He seemed strangely relieved that I would unburden him from the full weight of taking care of her heart. I felt good about the conversation, and I pondered, "This is the way the brother/sister relationship should be—where we can share questions, opinions and spur one another on so we can understand God and each other better."

But the more I thought about it, the more I suspected that there was more going on. I just knew he was talking about me. I thought it was interesting since he was the one who complained about girls misinterpreting him all the time. If he was concerned about initiating interaction with me, maybe I needed to make it easier on him.

CHAPTER 8

After hearing that he was interested in someone, my Shane radar worked on overdrive. Sensitive to anything he did or said, I noticed one day that he seemed upset. Concerned about him, I wanted to let him know without being too obvious. So I wrote a little note and stuck it under his door.

Ten minutes later, Shane called. "Would you come here, please?"

Imagining his glowing response to my word of encouragement, I walked over to his dorm room. I was sure he appreciated my note. I knocked on the door, and he asked me to come in.

I caught my breath as I opened the door and saw him sitting on the edge of his bed, holding my note with a concerned look on his face. "I thought we talked about this. Is this a problem for us?"

"No!" I denied. My flushed cheeks must have given me away.

"This *is* a problem for us, isn't it? I really thought you were safe since we had already discussed it." He was visibly annoyed.

Words could hardly form in my humiliated mind, so I simply uttered, "I'm sorry," and as quickly as I could, I put the door between us again and hightailed it for my room.

I was never so embarrassed in all of my life. There was no easy recovery that would allow me to save face. I felt naked and ashamed. How could I possibly allow myself to feel something for him when he explicitly told me not to?

Marion found me a few minutes later and asked what was wrong. I couldn't imagine myself admitting my failure to anyone else. I could barely get it out with her.

"A couple weeks ago, Shane told me that girls always think that he is interested in them. He wanted to be sure that wasn't a problem for us. I didn't think it was, until he started to talk to me about the fact that he was interested in someone here. He asked for my advice and I started to wonder if he might be talking about me. Today I took a note to his room to encourage him, and he called me out on it. I cannot believe it! I had no intention of being foolish like every other girl who thought he liked them!"

I buried my head in my hands and cried, "I am 'that girl'!"

Then Marion spoke some of the most powerful words I'd ever heard. "Andrea, you are a human being. Of course you had feelings for him!"

But I didn't want to be a human being. I was special. I was strong. I was not the foolish giggly girl to be written off by a man. I wanted to crawl into a hole and never come back out.

I couldn't avoid him. Nor could I ignore the cracks left in my self-image. I hated my inability to fit into the ideal me I had created for myself.

I say things like "I think girls are crazy," and then I act like one! The situation rolled around in my mind for the next few days.

Marion says I'm human, but what does it mean to be human? And why am I so opposed to it?

Over the course of a few months at seminary, I was undone. Having opened my heart up so that I began to find out who I really was deep down, what I saw was terrifying to me. I saw profound weakness, longing and doubt. Everything I had thought I was fell down around me, and I was totally exposed in the rubble of my own storm. So I penned this song.

Where am I? I thought I was moving.
I ran with all the strength I could stand.
Now You say, I've been going nowhere,
I feel my feet sinking in sand.

This image in front of me shows me I'm weak.
I don't want to see this broken body.

Who am I? I thought I was someone,
I had much to offer the world.
Now You say, I've been helping no one,
Agenda's dismantled, unfurled.

This image in front of me shows me I'm weak,
I don't want to see this broken heart bleed.

I've been runnin' and searchin' for something I've known,
Breaking through all that's new to find my way home,
And all that surrounds me is all that remains
Of the storm that keeps blowin' through
And calls out my name.

Why am I craving a feeling? A memory my mind can't recall.
Deep within, my body is trembling,
Are there no answers at all?

This vision that moves me reminds me I'm weak,
But I can't cease hoping for the comfort I seek.

I've been runnin' and searchin' for something I've known
Breaking through all that's new to find my way home
And all that surrounds me is all that remains
Of the storm that keeps blowin' through
And calls out my name.

When I found out that my carefully planned image was blown, it took me a while to recover from the shock. But when I did, I recognized that I was hurting myself and others by living to achieve validation and favor. Looking at the world through new eyes, I saw how my shame-driven strategy to keep "the real me" hidden and to project a pressured "ideal me" didn't work.

It's not like anyone had told me when I was a kid that I had to be a good girl. They didn't need to; I paid attention to everything. And I really believed I could be whatever I decided to be. So I constructed my own identity, based on what I believed it would take for God to smile at me and then to use me to change the world.

There was something about this storm that was destructive to everything I'd constructed in my own strength. It shattered my ideals, but it exposed my truth. And the truth was that there was nothing I could do to make God love me more or less. I was no more special to God because of anything I had or hadn't done. He loved me right in the midst of pain, weakness and longing. He loved me no matter how much I blessed or hurt Him and others. God's love and forgiveness were constant because Jesus – not my own performance – was the basis for my relationship with God.

It astounded me! That storm that "keeps blowing through" kept deconstructing the image I had believed to be true about myself, and I was left feeling completely exposed - weak, emotional and not nearly as "good" as I thought I was. But it seemed to be calling out my name and stirring in me a longing for a memory my mind couldn't recall, something I knew deep down but hadn't experienced yet. I wanted more connection and more purpose. I wanted something deeper, more real and powerful than I'd experienced before. And somehow it felt possible.

The new, experiential awareness that I was just like everyone else released me from the chains I'd placed on myself to be my optimal self all of the time. It freed me to stop pretending and stop forcing myself to be what I thought I needed to be. I didn't need to be anything in particular anymore. What I needed was Jesus.

Once my cover was blown, everything changed, and there was no going back. It was time to throw off my self-protection and see what it was like to take real relational risks.

I am who and what I am because that is God's perfect plan for me. I don't need to change my personality. He made me with these gifts, this intellectual capacity, this heart and calling, for a reason. I need to be who God created me to be.

"Thank You, God. Thank You for making me the way that I am. I'm sorry for doubting You. Thank You for giving me many gifts, talents, and passions - leadership, initiative and sensitivity. Thank You for making me a woman."

There was a lesson I had learned from holding in grief for five years: grief never just leaves. I couldn't master my emotions by acting stronger than they were to muscle them away. More than that, I needed to honestly acknowledge them, even if they made me feel weak. *Maybe my abilities aren't so bad after all.*

I began taking midnight prayer walks, asking God to fill me and move in the people around me. Sometimes it seemed that there were only a few of us who could see the hurt running around campus. Most people did nothing more than keep up with their studies, let alone think about people outside of their immediate peer group. They didn't have time or energy to acknowledge other people's pain.

Marion and I were willing to see the heartache around us. We didn't necessarily want to, but we were willing. When I thought back through the years, I realized most people didn't want to know the depths of the problems others faced. Perhaps they were afraid it would depress them or that they might feel responsibility to make everything better. But that wasn't how I felt, for some reason. I saw the pain and believed that it was possible that their good dream could be shattered in order to replace it with an appetite for something better. I believed God would move in the other person through their brokenness and pain.

The problem I had faced prior to that point was that I had believed I needed to be good, strong and right all of the time in order to really please God. I saw the instructions in the Bible as a shortcut to God. If I refrained from whatever He wanted me to refrain from and even more, He would be pleased with me. If I did whatever I was supposed to do and even more, I would be important to Him. I created myself a beautiful little box to fit into so I could control other people's perception of me and make God happy. But the box was also a barrier. It kept me from truly connecting with others, and I didn't realize that. My beautiful little box just didn't know what to do with the messiness of relationships.

I had wondered why it seemed so many people didn't want to know me for who I was. The fact that I could get people to share about themselves, yet I didn't really feel connected to them, had disturbed me. If they didn't want to receive my advice, I had assumed it was because their hearts were hard. Concluding it was because they didn't want to grow or know God more deeply, I had no idea that it had way more to do with me than it did with them.

My advice was generally not bad advice; my care for others was not disingenuous. But my understanding of myself was incomplete. I tried to cut to the chase and make the right decisions in my life without considering first what was true about my own heart. It left me feeling like I could be close to God without relating well with other people. Believing I had a shortcut to holiness that skipped the heart and went right to actions, I wanted others to find it, too.

But not anymore. Once I realized that God loved the real me, right where I was, I wanted to help others find the truth about themselves, too. My tendency to be an interviewer and extract hidden thoughts and feelings from others needed to be replaced with a genuine curiosity that offered others a welcome space to explore and share themselves with me. At last, I too wanted to reach the world with God's love, for the sake of the Gospel.

CHAPTER 9

In the middle of November, a couple friends and I warmed ourselves by the fire at a rustic coffee shop. Another guy from seminary was there. We chatted with Thomas a bit before he told us about his church in the city and invited us to come. The idea of leaving my comfort zone in the suburbs scared me, but I was ready to take a leap of faith. The next Sunday, I joined him and his friend for a trip into Chicago to go to church.

Park Community Church was meeting at a ballroom in Lincoln Park that summer. Chairs circled around a makeshift stage under a grand chandelier, and vibrant city people filled the room. The first night I visited was a night of testimonies. They had been working through Rick Warren's book *The Purpose Driven Life* as a church, and on this night people had the opportunity to share how they were changing. A tall, dark, handsome man stood up and stated, "I am a lawyer, but after going through this book, I believe God made me to be a healer. I'm going to quit my job and go to med school."

Are you kidding?! I couldn't believe the things I was hearing about the way God seemed to be moving in these people. I met a comedian, a Romanian real estate agent who was also a musician, and a Swiss man who was writing a 1 Corinthians commentary. I was fascinated. We attended a group for 20-somethings that met after the church service.

There was an energy there that I was not used to seeing. The people in the group lived in a culture that was very different than the one I was used to. If they wanted to be Christians, they had to decide if they would flow with the culture around them or head upstream. These were not the kind of people who wanted to take the easy path. They were thirsty for fellowship, and Park Community Church was their drinking well.

This church may be just what I need. I've been praying that God would broaden my understanding and experience. Could He really have provided the means to that here?

I also enjoyed getting to know the guy from seminary who had let me tag along. It was interesting to encounter someone else willing to process everything in depth. I chuckled when Thomas said that he had so many passions and things he wanted to do in life. I could relate. I definitely wanted to go back with them to the church in the city.

A couple days later, I was typing away in the computer lab when a man wearing a brown fedora slumped down next to me and said, "Hey."

"Hi," I smiled at Thomas. I was relieved at how easy he made it for me to act casually rather than having to call him on the phone, out of the blue. "I had a great time at your church on Sunday. I would love to go back next week after Thanksgiving break."

"Cool," he lit up in response. "My small group is going to a poetry slam that night, so I thought I would go into the city for church in the morning, hit a coffee shop to study during the afternoon and then meet them later."

I hadn't realized it was going to be such a big day. "Oh, I don't want to intrude on your group time." I'd also had no idea why they would want to go somewhere to listen to poetry. It sounded boring to me.

"No, you should come!" he insisted. "If you're going to start coming to church down there, you need to meet my small group anyway."

That chilly Sunday morning, the two of us headed downtown for church. As the shadows on the grey horizon turned into towering skyscrapers, I mused that this trip felt a lot more like a date than a day of church activities.

We found out at church that no one else was going to the poetry slam that night, but Thomas thought we should still go. It was dark when we headed toward uptown. The street walls narrowed as he explained his excitement.

"We're going to The Green Mill. It's this really cool, old bar that used to be run by the mafia."

He must have heard my heart start to pound my chest. *What had I agreed to?*

"Oh, don't worry. It's all safe now. But back in the '20's, Al Capone and his men went there all the time." He looked like a little boy about to unwrap a huge Christmas present.

A trip to The Green Mill was definitely something I wouldn't have done on my own, but it sounded exciting. "OK. So you said they read poetry there? In this really cool bar?" It was hard for me to imagine.

"It's not just poetry. It's a poetry slam. I don't know how to explain it, but it's really cool. I promise. This is where the poetry slam movement really got going. Now there are slams all over the world."

Obviously this place was a big deal. We found a parking spot on the dark street a couple blocks away. Buildings crowded in on us as I restrained myself from looking over my shoulder every few feet. At least I was with a guy who used to play football. We walked up to the unassuming hole in the wall. Light bulbs protruded from the green sign, indicating we were at The Green Mill. I held my breath and squared my shoulders, not sure if I wanted to walk in first or let Thomas clear the path for me. I chose to hold back.

A step in the door was a step back in time. Beer mist hung in the air, accompanied by a sweet jazz vibe that had my body grooving past the old bar and into the seating area. Step. Step-a-step. The rounded, green felt booth we sat in took up two of the more than twenty foot width of the tavern. Knowledge of the underground tunnels used by the mob had my imagination running and my eyes scanning the walls for bullet holes that could have come from the gun of Al Capone. Our booth sat under an eight-foot horizontal painting of ships on the water, framed by a melodramatic six inches of thick, rounded wood another inch deep. I felt vulnerable and small, yet something about just being in this place made me feel cool. Uptown.

A man with a big string bass plucked a beat while a guitar ran a groove over the top. A woman came to the small stage and started speaking rhythmically. Or was she singing? The music kept going, and her words slipped out to a laid back beat. Thomas and I looked at each other. I shook my head in amazement while he nodded his.

"I can't believe I'm here right now," I said as I turned back to watch the woman amp up her voice and nearly yell out words that made us feel her pain when she was ignored on the train by a white man in his suit coat.

A man with dark curls three inches deep around his head stood up as he raised his hand. He swaggered up to the stage and informed us that he was going to share a poem he had written that morning. He started to speak, and the musicians picked up his vibe. It dawned on me that they had no idea where his poem was going; they were just feeling it and instantly matching his rhythm, intensity and tone with their jazz accompaniment.

The men and women on stage that night held nothing back. They unearthed their emotional core and unleashed it in all-out self-expression. I'd never before witnessed anything like it.

I wondered if I would ever be able to express myself like people of The Green Mill Poetry Slam.

. . . .

CHAPTER 10

. . . .

I came back from Christmas break wondering where things were headed with Thomas. In spite of appreciating how he invited me out of my comfort zone, I never felt so ignorant as I did when with him. I was comfortable asking questions to allow him to go deeper in conversation. But then he wanted me to respond so it would be more of a dialogue. I wasn't sure how to respond when I'd never before considered the things he was talking about. Uncertain about what to say, I started to feel foolish around him.

The next time we went into the city for church, I insisted that I drive. Perhaps being in the driver's seat would give me the leverage I needed to speak more assertively with him. Thomas seemed to have issues with his height, so, up to that point, I had been careful not to wear tall shoes. But not this day! I needed a power play to give me confidence, so I wore boots with a 2-inch heel. It worked. I felt more like myself, and it showed.

On our drive back, I got gutsy and shared about my newfound comfort in admitting my human weaknesses. I played my theme song *This Is Me*, by Faith Hill, a personal declaration of identity, claiming imperfections and vulnerable feelings.

"You mean, you want to be like everyone else?" Thomas was surprised at how I related to the lyrics.

"Yes! For so long I felt like I was closer to God than everyone else, and I didn't even realize I felt that way. It was like I was on one side of a pane of glass with God, looking in on the world."

He leaned into the strobe of light and dark as we passed street lamps on the freeway. I continued, "It was lonely. But I didn't want to be like other girls who are written off for their emotions. I wanted to be strong so I could be respected for my ideas. I refused to want anything I didn't already have because admitting my longings made me vulnerable to disappointment. Vulnerable to other people who might reject me."

"What is it that you long for that makes you so vulnerable?"

Here's where the rubber meets the road, Andrea. Will you own it or not?

"Marriage and kids," I admitted. "I want to connect deeply with someone. The fact that I'm not married leaves me longing for it and vulnerable to the pain of not having it…of being rejected."

I swallowed hard. Did I just say that?

Thomas nodded his head and seemed to be thinking. "I want to find someone who is independent. Someone who can take care of themselves and think for themselves."

I stared at the white dashes, holding my car on the road. Was I relieved or nervous to realize that he wanted an independent thinker?

Maybe there are men who can handle strong women. Girls like me need to hear that.

Thomas and I talked frequently once classes started up for the spring semester. Late one January afternoon, I was napping in my dorm room when I heard a knock on the door.

Still groggy, I sat up in bed and smoothed my hair. I assumed it was Marion or one of the other women on my floor. "Come on in."

Thomas walked in and pulled his fedora off his head, "Hey. What are you up to?"

Masking my surprise and diminishing the expression of my pleasure that he would seek me out, I admitted that I'd been taking a nap. I offered him my desk chair, the only one in the room.

"Thanks. So how was your day?" he forced.

How was your day? Why is he here? There's something going on.

I cooperated with the uncharacteristically light conversation and soon realized the flushing of his face.

"I came here because I needed to tell you something."

I caught my breath and attempted to appear composed. "OK. What's up?"

He looked down at his hat, dancing nervously from one hand to the other. "I wanted to let you know that last summer I made a commitment to God that I would fast from dating for a year, and I intend to keep that promise."

"OK," I managed. I could be mature about it. "Do we need to set any boundaries to be sure that happens?"

Why does a guy decide to fast from dating? I have no desire to be added to some list of girls he's dated. I don't want to be one in a long line of many.

"No. Things are fine the way they are," he supposed.

Somehow his vulnerability empowered me to speak. "Well, if I need boundaries, I'll let you know."

The hat stood still, mid-dance, and he looked right at me, eyes a little wider than they had been when he was speaking. He almost stumbled over his agreement, "OK." After shaking off what appeared to be shock that I might need boundaries, he started extolling the virtues of fasting. I got the feeling he was suggesting I ought to fast from dating as well. "Restraining from something that would otherwise be easy to enjoy can reap huge benefits."

It was my turn. "I haven't dated in six years. I think I've restrained long enough."

Thomas's head jolted to the side, "Oh. I guess you have. Well, I'll let you get back to your nap. See you later." And he left the room.

It felt like we'd broken up, yet were we supposed to continue everything just as it had been? I was more confused than ever. He didn't say he wasn't interested in me; he just said he couldn't date. We were on a trajectory for relational collision, and yet he claimed he didn't think our interactions needed to change. Part of me wished he had just said he wasn't interested. I knew what that was like. The situation reminded me of the first time Shane told me that he liked talking to me but that he wasn't interested in me.

What am I, just a counselor for men? They seem to want me for great conversation, but they aren't interested in me as a woman.

We proceeded as if nothing happened, spending an increasing amount of time together. I kept wondering what he was really thinking. He certainly still seemed to be interested in me and kept inviting me to run errands, help with projects, and hang out with groups of people. A couple of weeks later, there was a three-day stretch of time when we didn't see each other, and I started to wonder if it were all a dream.

Am I reading him right or just hallucinating? He values my support, but is it just because I'm safe? No girl wants to be the safe friend. No girl wants to be emotionally intimate like a mother. I certainly don't. I love talking to him, being with him, keeping up with him but I don't want to do it if we're not exploring the possibility of doing life together.

The next Sunday on the way to church we had a conversation about me. I was completely uncomfortable as he asked questions and probed deeper into my psyche. "You're like a sprinter in conversation. You go really fast for a little bit and then close up."

Here you go again, Andrea...looking like a fool in front of this guy. Why can't you be yourself with him?

He went on, "You say you want to connect, but when I keep asking questions and you're about to say something real, you freeze up."

Was I trembling? I stared at the road, relieved I didn't have to look at him. "I guess I'm not used to people asking those questions. Most people don't want to go into those deeper places with me." I felt the urge to start crying, but I choked back the tears. I didn't know when I'd actually told someone that.

He didn't seem to believe me. "What about counseling? Did you ever have a counselor that asked questions like that?"

"I've never been to counseling." Up to that point, I hadn't thought that was strange at all.

"You haven't? How can you study counseling when you've never been to counseling?" he wondered.

My thoughts were beginning to take off, so I pulled the reins. *That's a fair question.*

"Well, I've always wanted to connect deeply with people, but it seems most people are either scared of it or don't know how to do it. So I guess I try to ask them questions and let them share the deeper parts of themselves. I guess I thought that was the only way to do it. As for me, I journal. I think and pray through my own emotional processing and then I tell people about it later."

No wonder I feel like I'm on the other side of a window from everyone else. My inner life is larger than life and completely separate from other people. I don't know if I can share like he wants me to share.

I thought I was a brutally honest person, but this conversation revealed that perhaps I wasn't willing to be as transparent as I thought I was. Maybe I was scared of it. I continued to ponder this.

I have always craved deep intimacy, but others seem scared of it, so I let them draw the boundary lines. I'll go as far as they'll let me. But I rarely move beyond sharing what I already know because I find that people don't really want to know. They don't push further. And though I have great friends who sometimes do probe deeper, a lack of time and energy get in the way. We often stop conversations before they are really finished, probably because I could go on forever.

There Thomas was, prodding and touching my heart in places that no one else had ever tried to reach, wanting me to tell him that he was capable of doing what no one else could do. But sharing or admitting that would require a level of vulnerability that I just wasn't sure I could offer. I was afraid that he would expose me and then leave like Shane, that I would open myself up and he would let me go. I wanted to share my real, in-time thoughts with someone else, but I wasn't sure if I should open myself up to Thomas because he wasn't pursuing a relationship.

When is it time to open up and let it go with someone and when should I hold back? I feel like I'm on the edge of a cliff, sameness behind me, change in front of me, and all I can do is jump. How I land is completely up to God, and I have to trust him with it. It's not an easy thing to do. Is Thomas going to break my heart?

CHAPTER 11

I was on high alert after Thomas told me we couldn't date. I'd been in this position before and though the outcome was good for me, I wasn't interested in additional humiliation. But our continued interaction had me wondering what was really going on.

Then one day I latched onto a nugget of hope in my Marriage and Family Counseling class. Dr. Bryan Maier shared a diagram he'd developed through his experience and as a way to explain something many counselors had said through the years. It outlined a path through the typical stages in marriage. "I adore you" was up high and to the left. Then, after a steep slope down low, he wrote, "I hate you." A steady slope back up included the words "I like you," and then finally, "I love you."

Dr. Maier said that often, when we fall in love, we adore one another. And as long as that adoration lasts, couples feel like they are on a high. But it is as if they make an unconscious prenuptial agreement to remain there. "If you do not continue to make me feel as amazing as I feel when we fell in love, I reserve the right to…divorce or complain or nag or withdraw."

Then when life hits, as it might in the first year of marriage or when they have their first child, and a couple realizes they aren't complying with the unspoken agreement, they are disillusioned. They feel like they've fallen out of love and even hate each other for breaking the promise of adoration. Many couples never get past that stage because it feels like the end of the relationship.

But a couple dedicated to making the marriage work eventually gets to the point where they can stand one another again and can even say, "I like you." Still, some couples never move beyond that stage. It is the couple that continues to work to build their life together, aligning their goals and meeting trials arm-in-arm, that eventually comes to a point where they can earnestly and honestly say, "I love you" from the depths of their heart.

The diagram concept intrigued me. How should I proceed with this knowledge? He said these were the typical stages of marriage, but since when was I typical? Why couldn't I skip over the first three stages and go straight to the "I love you" stage? I had a map of the path, so why not fly to the end instead of treading the difficult ground in the middle?

Does falling in love need to occur at all? How else am I supposed to know that I've found "the one"? Is it really all just a choice?

It wasn't the first time I thought I could rise above the norm. I'd been assessing the pathways to various outcomes all my life. Girls who giggle were written off for being emotional, so I didn't giggle. Girls who fuss over their appearance were considered vain, so I didn't fuss. People who date without marriage in mind get hurt, so I didn't date just to date. And when I had slammed my heart shut six years before, I determined to skip over the hardest parts of relationships. I figured that if I knew the outcome I desired, I could achieve it without getting my hands dirty.

What if I could skip to "I love you" by taking my heart out of the game from the beginning and assessing my relationships analytically? Then I wouldn't get tricked. If I never adored my husband, I wouldn't have to hate him either. I could skip to the "like" phase and work my way to "love." Or could I?

In early February, Thomas called: "I wanted to know if you see us romantically. Because if you do, we need to address that."

I felt like I'd heard this before. *Is he throwing me under the bus?*

I wasn't sure of his intent, but I was relieved that we were finally addressing our relationship. I feigned as much confidence as I could, "Well, yes. I think that there is potential there for that." Vague was as close to admitting my feelings as I intended to get. The phone receiver nearly slipped out of my anxiety-drenched hand.

"Well, I am still committed to not dating until this summer, but if we keep our relationship from getting physical, I think we can keep talking to see if we are headed in the same direction."

"OK." I wasn't all that disappointed that he wanted to refrain from physical contact, but I wondered how a couple could keep from touching for four months? Was it possible? Was it wise?

"You should know that I'm just looking for red flags. That's the only thing that I think would keep us from making a commitment to each other this summer."

Standing at my dresser, phone receiver in hand, I shivered. Was this excitement or fear? I wasn't sure. But I could hardly breathe. Maybe this was God giving me the opportunity to fly like a bird, straight to "I love you."

Our new arrangement had me thinking that perhaps we found the perfect short cut on the marriage diagram. Thomas seemed to have a checklist he needed to get through to be sure I didn't turn out to be full of red flags. One of those important items on his list seemed to be that I shared his core passion for a dissatisfaction with the Christian culture. He had never said anything I really disagreed with, so I made sure not to wave a red flag in front of his face. I could be dissatisfied, too.

One night we hung out with my good friend Trisha and her husband Joe. Joe was studying to be a pastor, and Trisha was an incredibly supportive wife. She and I grew up together, and they were instrumental in getting me to come to seminary in the first place.

It hadn't occurred to me before, but my relationship with Thomas was built entirely on his turf. I was excited to be introducing him to a small patch of my own.

But I realized something was off from the moment we stepped in the door. My friends engaged him in conversation, but his answers were shorter than usual. Trisha and I talked of the good old days growing up in Nebraska, but, rather than showing interest, it seemed that Thomas was simply enduring our banter.

When we left, he admitted his discomfort in the situation. I wondered - how could we have such great mental chemistry and yet have completely different experiences of people important to me? Clearly, something was wrong.

Who am I? Am I myself with him, or am I giving him the answers he wants so I don't raise any red flags?

My heart sank. He was looking for something specific, and I was trying to be what he was looking for.

"Thomas, I think I've been holding back with you."

"What do you mean?"

"Well, I have more thoughts and opinions than you realize. But I don't know how to share them with you. For some reason, when we talk, I clam up. You seem like you know exactly what you think about things, and I don't necessarily disagree. But you are so incredibly passionate about your dissatisfaction with the Christian culture, and the truth is that I don't feel it as intensely as you do. It's like I'm this twig starting to grow, and you're a full-blown tree. Are you OK with that?"

My heart rate could have powered a kitchen appliance. *This could be it. The red flag I've been trying so hard not to wave.*

Steam seemed to be rising from his fedora. "I can be OK with that. But this is a lot to think about." After thirty minutes hashing things out, we decided to continue our conversation another day.

He must have wondered who in the world I was if I weren't being real with him. I wondered how I was supposed to be independent and yet still agree with him about everything.

He called me a couple of days later and asked me to meet him in the lounge. I walked out of my room, determined to be as unapologetically "me" as I could be. Apparently I was more sassy that day than I realized.

He invited me to sit down across from him. "So I wanted to tell you what happened this weekend."

"OK." I refused to worry as I looked him right in the eye. I wasn't used to feeling so confident with him.

"Last night I asked God to reveal to me if this was 'it' or not. Then this morning I woke up with a panic attack."

What?! I scare him? Does he have any idea how frightened I've been every moment of this relationship?

I didn't voice my displeasure at being the cause of his panic attack, so he continued, "I felt a lot better when I realized that we weren't stuck in this relationship. We can go on or end it, either way. That was freeing."

Oh, that's comforting.

He went on, unaware of my sarcastic thoughts. "I've also been thinking about how you said you aren't as passionate about your dissatisfaction with the Christian culture as I am. I know I said that was OK the other night, but the more I think about it, the more it bothers me." Just saying those words seemed to leave a bad taste in his mouth.

Just what I've always wanted...to disgust the man I'm seeing.

"So I called you down here to let you know all of this and ask – where do you see us now?"

Without missing a beat, I answered, "It sounds like we're really good friends, Thomas."

His eyes opened wide, "I didn't come here to break up, but I thought my experience was significant, and I wanted your take on it."

I smiled gently and stated, "No, I think we need to take a step back. I know what I'm worth, and I don't want to be in a relationship where I'm not wanted for who I am."

All of a sudden, I realized how badly I had wanted to say that. It was so freeing. I hadn't tried to be the old ideal Andrea with him, but I hadn't been speaking up with the real me either. I had kept quiet to be sure he wouldn't have the chance to reject me for who I was, but when I began to speak up, he obviously didn't like it.

But the more I thought about it, the more I wondered what it was that I really did want him to know about me? Why was it so hard to articulate the real me?

What is my identity? I'm sick of hearing that my identity is found in Christ. What does that mean anyway? I am still more than that. What makes me different from every other Christian? If it's what I do, then I'm changing all the time, and I will either be devastated because I fail or prideful because I succeed. My identity can't be about what I do.

I knew one thing. I wouldn't be able to know who I was or what I wanted to share if I tried to be someone's ideal woman. As much as we wanted to honor God and each other, neither Thomas nor I were clear about who we were or what we wanted in a relationship.

We thought we could skip over the hard stuff. Maybe by breaking up, we had.

I needed a breath of fresh air, so, when a young woman I was mentoring invited me to her home in Green Bay for the weekend, I eagerly accepted. She was going to be playing her violin in a band for a worship concert, and I was excited to hear her play.

I would be making the three-hour trip on my own, so I packed a book on tape that my grandparents had sent to me. Todd Beamer was a passenger on Flight 83 on 9/11. His story became famous after a 911 dispatcher shared the conversation she had had with him just before he and other passengers attacked the terrorists on their plane. It crashed into a field in Pennsylvania, presumably saving the White House and many more lives. *Let's Roll* was the story of Todd and Lisa Beamer, as told by Lisa. I popped tape after tape into my car's player and soaked in Lisa's words.

The way she described her husband made me cry as I rolled down the interstate. Their relationship sounded like it was full of mutual respect and love and real connection. How tragic that she could taste it for only a few years and then lose it! I wondered if the fulfillment she had experienced in marriage was worth the hole left in her heart after losing it. She seemed to say that it was worth all the pain.

I needed to hear it. For so long I had attempted to deny the intensity with which I longed for a great marriage. Lisa had had it, and now she longed for it. Maybe longing for it wasn't the sign of weakness that I thought it was. Maybe longings are part of being human, and it was OK to feel their pain.

I sat by myself at the worship concert, wondering if I would ever taste the intimacy and respect that Todd and Lisa Beamer shared. Kim's sweet violin resonated with my soul in tones of desire as I closed my eyes and honestly prayed from my heart.

"Lord, I want someone to put his arm around me as though I belong with him. I want someone to look at me as though he sees my heart and

adores me anyway. I want the intimacy and respect Lisa had with Todd. I want...." A thought inspired by my theology class interrupted the flow of my honest confession.

"*God, I know in my head that perfect intimacy with You is better than intimacy with another human could ever be, but I don't feel it in my heart.*" Then a wave of understanding washed over me, releasing gentle sobs.

"*This! This is what You want me to know! This longing I have for a person is real, but it is the same longing I have for You. I just didn't know it! You love me better than a man ever could. YOU put your arm around me as though I belong to You. YOU see my heart and adore me anyway!*"

I came away from that worship concert strangely weakened and then empowered by my human needs once more. It finally made sense in my whole body that every desire and every fulfillment of that desire was worth feeling. I could feel every bit of longing for things of this world and then look up and say,

"*I certainly long for someone to put his arm around my shoulder, but that same longing is what YOU fulfill with Your love for me. Honestly feeling the pain of longing helps me grasp what it is that Your love truly fulfills in me! I can enjoy the pleasures of this world and say, 'YOU are even better than this!'*"

Knowing in my bones that God was the fulfillment of my desires didn't stop me from desiring deep connection with other people. It freed me to own it. I wasn't using relationships to fill my desire for God; they were a living, breathing example of how I much I wanted Him.

And for the first time I could tremble with conviction and say, "This world is not my home. But I will live here with every fiber of my being." I couldn't wait to tell the world!

I understood for the first time what it really looked like to be weak, fragile and vulnerable. Weak was my new strong. Though I felt pain and longing, at least it was real, unburdened by shame or pressure.

Though I wanted to share the revolution in my heart with other people, I found it difficult to describe. "I want to throw a big party with balloons and dancing and great celebration!" I truly did. And though people smiled genuinely when I told them of my transformation, I still got the sense that if I expressed my joy to the degree that I knew I could, it would be too much for other people. So I found other ways of expressing my delight.

Late at night, when all of the serious seminary students were locked in their rooms studying or sleeping, I locked myself up in the commons area. I sat down at the old piano that hadn't seen a tuning fork in many years, and I pulled out a book of songs by Cindy Morgan. I plunked away, thankful no one was around, and the songs filled the little room. It felt good to sing my heart out.

I couldn't sing like that in chapel or church. I certainly couldn't do it in my dorm room. But late at night, when it was just me and the piano, I could sing the song in my heart. I'd never felt so free.

When no one was around, it was much easier to admit the truth about myself. I realized that God loved me no matter what. It was like being on my childhood swing where I could honestly express my heart to Him again, only more richly. I was safe to bring what was in the dark into the light of His love. I found such freedom there, such power. I felt raw, real and alive. My heart was tender, but the alternative was hardness. I'd rather feel the gamut of emotions than contain them.

CHAPTER 12

For months I chipped away at the image I had created of the ideal Andrea, and I began rejecting the methods I'd used to guard my heart from pain. I felt raw and wondered what else I could possibly learn.

My summer intensive course proved my transformation was far from over. I came to Group Counseling class pretty confident about my ability to lead groups of people in transformational processes. I'd led a number of Bible studies and small groups for all ages of people, and at the time I was co-leading a small group of women for the twenty-somethings group at my church in the city. Knowing how to listen and ask great questions that invited people to dig in and explore their hearts more deeply, I was convinced I had a lot I could offer groups of people as a friend, facilitator and teacher.

Unfortunately for my ego, one of the requirements of the class was that we actually participate in group counseling. At the time, the picture in my mind of group counseling was of people sitting around a circle taking turns breaking down and crying. I had never participated in counseling or group counseling up to this point. One thing I was sure of, I had no intention of being tricked into breaking down and crying in the group.

Then one day it happened. Tears began to form in my eyes, and my group saw it.

I almost had my eyes dry when a woman in her thirties asked, "What are the tears for, Andrea?"

Her question called them out again. "I don't know." I refused to look at anyone. My terror was choking me so all I could imagine was gently excusing myself and walking out the door. "I don't want to do this."

A kind gentleman wanted to relieve me of my discomfort. "It's OK. You don't have to share."

Our instructor came out from behind the viewing glass and knelt down beside the classmate who was leading us at the time. He coached her on how to handle the situation. My dread increased; there was no way he would let me walk out.

Out of the corner of my blurry eye, I saw him whisper to the leader. She spoke up, "Let's stay with this feeling, Andrea. What are you feeling right now?"

I had no words to describe what I was feeling. I almost imperceptibly shook my bowed head. "I don't know."

Someone else didn't believe me. "Is it that you don't know or that you don't want to tell us?"

There was no stopping my tears now. All I could do was place my hands as a barrier between me and the group. I completely covered my face. "I really don't know. I can't do this!"

I pictured myself in the group from a bird's eye view, breaking down and crying. The reality of that ridiculous image irritated me. "THIS IS SO CLICHÉ!" I growled.

The facilitator continued to invite me out of my shell, but I wouldn't budge. I'd made a big enough fool out of myself. I honestly didn't know why I was crying, and I had no idea how they would be able to help me until I'd figured it out.

I slunk back to my summer home that evening. I was living with a friend in her little hotel room that had been converted into an apartment. She had pulled her loveseat out from the back wall to give me a nook for my air mattress and a few belongings. I grabbed my journal, popped my earphones in and hunkered down in my hiding place to ponder why the scene in group counseling bothered me so much.

The next day, I volunteered to go first. "I want to apologize for clamming up yesterday. I know the whole point of this class and the group is to open up and be willing to grow through it, but when it came down to it, I was terrified." It was a relief to share this revelation while completely composed.

I looked around at the six other people sitting around the circle. They seemed to be interested in what I had to say, so I kept going.

"I analyze a lot. I'm always thinking about how things are and the way I think they could be. I came into this class with this image of a woman breaking down crying, and I had no intention of being so foolish as to let that happen to me. I know that sounds horrible. I'm sorry."

Another young woman could relate. "I know what you mean. I also consider existential questions. Sometimes it's hard to know what I'm feeling when I'm thinking so theoretically."

"YES!" I agreed. I felt a rush of relief to be able to think through this issue out loud. "When I'm out in the world talking to people, I tend to be really present with them in their feelings, but I'm thinking analytically about other stuff. It's like in my head I'm pulled back from the world, looking at it through a pane of glass. I can engage with other people about their feelings, but I don't know what I'm feeling until I get by myself and take time to process my experiences and how they're making me feel."

"That sounds really lonely," someone stated.

Tears returned, and my pace slowed. "It is. I thought I'd come a long ways in my willingness to be honest about how I feel, but, when I was in class yesterday, I realized I couldn't do it with you all here. I had to go back home to figure it all out later."

"What if you allowed yourself to feel with us present? What would that be like for you?" the facilitator asked.

"I'm not sure I'm capable of doing that," I answered honestly.

"Andrea," the facilitator stopped me. "I think you have a choice to make right now. Do you want to explore this further with us, or have you given up on the idea that you could be present with us?"

Ugh. I hadn't thought of it like that. "I would like to explore it a little if you don't mind. But I feel bad taking up more time."

"We are offering to be with you. Why do you feel bad?" she questioned.

"Well, I'm not used to people being willing to do this with me. I feel like I should be the one listening, not asking for help."

"What's wrong with asking for help?"

"I guess I don't mind asking for help, but...." A sob rolled up from my belly and out my head. I thought about the conversation Thomas and I had had months before when he had told me that I drop the baton in conversation. He was willing to ask about me, but when I shared what I really thought, he rejected me. I didn't want to expose my heart to people I couldn't trust.

Who did I really trust, anyway? "I'm angry."

"What's the anger about?"

"OK. This is really hard for me to admit, but this is what I'm feeling right now." I couldn't believe what I was about to say. "I feel resentful toward you guys for being willing to explore my heart."

"Why?"

Through a rush of tears and in a crackling voice, I spilled the truth. "Because you're strangers! I want my friends and family to ask about my heart. I want to connect with them, not you!"

The silence in the room made a way for my sobs. A few moments later, someone asked, "So your friends and family don't explore your heart?"

I composed myself enough to answer. "Well, I think they think they do. But maybe I just want to share more than they're used to or comfortable with."

Maybe I don't know how to do it. Maybe I'm expecting too much. Maybe I'm too much.

CHAPTER 13

The revelation that I wanted more out of my relationships felt disconcerting. My longing went deeper and was more intense than I had realized. I didn't just want a man to put his arm around me and tell me I belonged, I wanted to be known and appreciated for who I was, not what I did.

My interior world was much greater than I could express in the exterior world around me. Why would anyone make the effort to really know me? Who was actually capable of not only seeing me, but engaging with me? I wondered if I was making it all too complicated.

Late in the summer, it was my turn to lead the lesson for our small group of twenty-somethings after church. The other leader found a fun spot in the balcony for us to gather. My mind and heart were full with all of the amazing revelations I'd been experiencing, and I longed to share these things with my new friends circled around me. Their eyes popped open wide as I had them flip through the Bible for particular passages that had changed my perspective about my identity and my understanding of the Gospel in everyday life. It was exciting to share how God had been moving in me, and they seemed interested to learn about it.

But apparently the intensity of my lesson was the last straw for my co-leader. She called me later that week to confront me about it. The conversation went something like this.

"Andrea, we need to talk about last Sunday."

"OK." I was still reveling in the joy of having shared my story, and I was happy to discuss it.

But her frustrated and determined tone caught me off guard. "That lesson was way over their heads. These girls are really new to church, and they don't have all of the background knowledge you have. We need to start with character and work our way toward helping them understand the Bible. You can't just throw a bunch of scriptures at them and expect them to understand."

"Oh. I didn't know you felt that way. I just wanted to share what God had been doing in me. I didn't expect them to understand everything, but I really felt led to share my story," I attempted to explain.

"You just kept going from passage to passage. We were flipping all over the Bible!" She sounded irritated with me. "I know that you know a lot, but we can't throw it all at them at once. Your lesson was overwhelming and too intense for this group."

I had no idea what to say. "Oh. I'm sorry. I didn't mean to do that."

"Well, let's just focus on character for a while. I have a book we can read and discuss as a group."

I hated reading books with groups or leading a group through someone else's Bible study. It was unclear to me if my repulsion at the thought was a rejection of authority or just the way I was made. But discussing someone else's thoughts felt like I was giving up on the possibility that my thoughts were worth discussing.

Not only were they not worthy of being discussed, perhaps they were destructive. Maybe I needed to be muzzled since I obviously had no idea when I was overwhelming everyone else.

But what good was I if I were too overwhelming to belong or make an impact on others? Why bother with the struggle of life if I couldn't make a difference in the world?

I needed advice, so I went to Marion. "I am really struggling right now in the tension between realizing my own sin and needing to be more bold in what I say.

"Andrea, you'll never have completely pure motives. 'Sin boldly,' as Martin Luther said. You can be aware of the complicated mix of sin and goodness inside of you and you can feel your weakness IF it drives you to the foot of the cross. That's where you'll find the grace of God. There's no room for self-pity there."

I couldn't find a happy place anymore, but I wondered if the foot of the cross would be the place I would find deeper joy.

The fall semester began after an entire year of intense struggle to explore my relationships, identity, ministry and theology. A new year was starting, but I was utterly exhausted. I felt like I'd been on an emotional roller coaster with sharp turns, fast loops, dips into deep waters and a hard fall at the end. I wanted to get off the ride, so I hid myself in my room, locked my door and laid my weary soul at the feet of popcorn, hot chocolate with marshmallows and easy to watch romantic comedies whenever I wasn't in class or in the dining hall.

My ideal self had broken down, and all that was left was real and raw. In my attempt to be honest, I couldn't muster a sense of confidence and purpose. I scraped away at anything that felt fake about me, having scratched enough to leave indentations on my soul. Pessimism infected my open wounds and spread through my being. Feeling very fragile,

I went to the one person whom I trusted with my delicate heart.

"Hello?"

"Hi, Mom," I fell into my bed and pressed the cell phone between my ear and the pillow.

"Well, hi! How are you doing?"

"Oh, I'm tired. How are you?" I wondered if she could sense my despondency.

"Well, honestly, it's been a rough day." She went on to tell me about three different people from my hometown with cancer, two of whom were on hospice by that point.

I held their families in my heart as I listened. How could anyone endure such pain and loss? How would I ever endure it? Hearing my mom's soothing, empathetic voice reminded me how much I missed the familiarity and comfort of home.

I curled up on my bed like I did when I was a child, barely hearing the news Mom spoke of from home. Darkness pressed in like a heavy cloud and gripped my heart as if it were threatening my very life.

"I just don't understand. I don't know how anyone could stand such loss. What is the point of all this anyway?"

"What do you mean, Andrea?"

"I mean – everything feels so hopeless right now. Like I am less and less capable of being happy. I just can't take this."

"It sounds like you need to pray about it, Andrea."

I didn't want to tell my mom how dark my prayers had become. "I do! Some nights I talk to God for hours, but I can't hear Him like I used to think I could."

I used to feel close to God, but when the window between me and the rest of the world shattered, the shards of glass seemed to sever my intimate connection with God, too.

Maybe I wasn't as close to God as I used to think I was. Maybe I couldn't trust Him like I used to. Or maybe He didn't trust me.

I longed to go home, but at the same time, I was afraid of home. If I went home, would I be giving up on the chance that I would ever get married? If I couldn't find a husband at seminary, how would I ever find someone to be a good match for me anywhere else?

I felt like a scattered little girl with an overactive thought life that I couldn't use for good. Not good that really counted for much, anyway.

I'm such a waste. On the outside I look like I'm questioning myself, my future and other people. But really I doubt God – His wisdom in creating me the way He did, that He really will use me, that my future is good.

Previously confident of my competence, now I started questioning all of my decisions. Being "real" made me face thoughts I didn't realize I'd had before. It was easy to avoid my doubts before, because the ideal Andrea was the ideal Christian – one that didn't doubt God at all. If I were being honest now, I had to admit that although I believed God could do anything, I wasn't sure He was good enough to make my intense existence worth it.

"Oh, God, please don't let me be a waste. Please don't let what I'm learning be only for me. Please let my life count. Draw me nearer and hold me closer right now."

Although I had come to seminary to find answers to the burning questions inside, after the most intense year of my life, I decided I didn't have answers. At last I was simply OK with the fact that I might never have answers.

This time had been important for finding out what I was capable of. At seminary, I realized that I wasn't the ideal Andrea I'd always wanted to be. The unfamiliar territory allowed me to explore what it meant to be human – to have longings and let those longings fuel my love instead of shaming me into holding it back. But I also realized that I couldn't run away from my fear that I might never connect deeply with others or make a lasting impact. I needed to keep trying. It was now time to go home.

SECTION THREE:
HIDING THE REAL ME

. . . .

CHAPTER 14

. . . .

That next semester I went home as an intern at my parent's church. My last degree requirement was to complete a practicum. Since I couldn't bear to think of leading someone else's program at a church, I, as usual, chose the unconventional approach and did a practicum project. I spoke with the pastor at my parents' church and asked if there were something I could provide them as an intern. He asked for a lay counseling program. I offered a class I called "Intentional Friendship."

That spring semester in Nebraska was spent synthesizing all I had learned in my classes and in my heart while I was in seminary. All of my experiences were woven together with what I had learned and came out as a curriculum to teach the foundation of intentional, healing relationships. I taught the class three times to over sixty women in their church. Dr. Maier, my supervising professor, chuckled at the excessive length of my 75-page thesis when it was complete. I was relieved to have the opportunity to think through the subject so thoroughly.

By the middle of that summer, I was ready to do something fun. My friend Brianne was home from Chicago, so we called up an old friend of mine who was a physical therapist in a nearby town. Aaron and I had met at an academic camp for local schools, back in high school. He was a really nice, but quiet guy. We'd stayed in touch off and on through the years. Thinking he might be available on the 4th of July, we invited him to spend the day with us.

We found a little spot next to a lake. When Aaron pursued a Frisbee I'd accidentally tossed in the wrong direction, it gave me a couple of minutes to say something I'd been thinking all day. "You know, Brianne, Aaron is a really good guy. I'm trying to marry him off!" Since they seemed to get along, I wondered if she would be interested in him.

"Oh, Andrea!" she laughed, tossing her mahogany curls behind her shoulder. "I don't know why you don't go for him!"

Aaron threw the disk back in our direction, and it was my turn to laugh. She wasn't the first person to suggest that Aaron and I get together, but I just didn't see it. He was quiet and seemed timid. I couldn't picture myself with someone who didn't keep up with me in conversation. Besides, he was a physical therapist, and, in my mind, physical therapists only married skinny runners. I definitely wasn't that.

That night Aaron and I sat on a blanket, fireworks falling around us, and he asked, "Do you think we have an impact on the people around us?"

"What do you mean?" Aaron and I had exchanged a number of emails regarding philosophical questions before, but it was still a little strange having him bring this up during a fireworks display.

"Well, we've been here all day playing games and eating, and I just wonder...did it really make a difference? Was it worth it?"

His intentional questions made me smile. I thought back through my friendship with him over the years. The first time I had seen Aaron, I'd thought he was a 6th grader at our high school academic camp and had wondered who had let a kid so young come to Summer Honors. It turned out that he was a rising sophomore in high school. A couple years and a few inches later, he called.

"Hi Andrea. How are you doing?... I wanted to ask if you would want to come with me to prom?"

"Oh! I feel so honored that you would ask!" I wasn't interested in Aaron romantically, but I definitely thought he was a neat guy.

As the president of his senior class, he attended the dinner by himself, and then he drove 45 minutes to pick me up. Although I was uncomfortable that he would spend so much time driving on prom night, he insisted. I slid into the seat of his white Chevy Lumina, and we made small talk. Twenty minutes into the drive, there was a long pause of silence. I wondered how the rest of the night would go if we couldn't keep up the conversation, but I decided not to worry about it.

Then he broke the silence. "So, what does your dad do for a living?"

I went along with it. "He's a financial planner. And my mom's a preschool teacher."

"Oh," he nodded. "I see." He was quiet again for a few seconds and seemed to be waiting for me to say something. I didn't get the hint, so he continued, "Well, I don't know if I told you, but my dad is a funeral director."

"Oh, wow. I didn't realize that! My dad used to sell monuments." I wasn't sure where to go with that information.

"Really?" He seemed to have more to say, "...and...we live in the funeral home."

"Oh, like the movie *My Girl?*" I didn't know what else to say without sounding scared and completely ignorant.

"Kind of." He paused again before the admission flew out, "So...we live in the funeral home. And the fireplace where we take pictures is across from where people lie in state for visitation."

I was totally blank. "OK."

"And..." he went on. "There's a guy there right now."

"A guy?" I wondered what he was trying to get at.

"Yes. In a casket."

I couldn't hold in the nervous burst of laughter that turned his gentle warning into a hilarious joke. He smiled and seemed relieved. "I just wanted to let you know before we got there."

When we walked into his home, I couldn't figure out what he was talking about. I smiled and stood beside him so his parents could take pictures, right in front of the fireplace, no casket in sight. The evening was enjoyable. He was a considerate date, but I didn't think much more about it after he brought me back home.

Eight years later, as we stared up at the fireworks on the 4th of July, I decided I wanted to consider Aaron. My initial impression of him had been incorrect. Words didn't come easily for him, but he wasn't timid. He persevered until he said what he intended to say, and usually what he wanted to say was rich with meaning. I respected that about him. I respected him.

I wondered if there were a possibility that I might stand with him in front of that fireplace for pictures again someday, casket or not. Maybe he was a real possibility, after all.

After a couple of months of Brianne, Aaron and me hanging out periodically, I had warmed up to the idea of Aaron and me. He lived 30 miles away, and we were both working, so it was difficult to foster our friendship without being intentional. My friend Brianne and I were desperate to enjoy life and relationships, so we found ways to get together.

I enjoyed being around Brianne and Aaron. Our friendships felt mutual and easy. We all seemed to enjoy doing things and talking together. I just wished Aaron would take more initiative and contact us every once in a while. But Brianne made getting together simple. She invited us to spend Labor Day with her family on their farm. I was sure Brianne knew I had a growing interest in Aaron at that point, yet somehow the two of them ended up on a 4-wheeler together, stuck in the mud. I looked down the hill, watching them work together to dig the utility vehicle out of the mud and found myself intensely jealous.

We see each other once every couple of weeks and then this happens to the two of THEM?!

They were a muddy mess when they finally got to the top of the hill. I was clean on the outside, but I was in shambles on the inside. I needed to get a grip on my mind and heart. I needed clarity about my relationship with Aaron. But I didn't want to ruin a perfectly good friendship with him by making subtle demands and forcing a discussion about whether or not he was interested in me. We had too much history to ruin it with a hasty "discuss the relationship" talk.

I recalled a time when I entered a relationship without knowing if I were truly interested in the guy. He initiated everything, and I went along because it was fun and I was curious. I waited until I knew we weren't a good match before I indicated anything was wrong. And by that point, I knew we needed to break up. By neglecting my own responsibility to determine my interest in him, I had led him on and let him down hard. It was one of my biggest regrets.

I had no intention of turning my friendship with Aaron into a regret. There were two things I needed to do in order to prevent that from happening: spend more time with Aaron and determine if I really were interested in him or if he were just another opportunity to daydream. But first, I needed advice.

I told my dad about the muddy 4-wheeler incident and admitted my jealousy. "What do you think I should do, Dad?"

"I think you need to find ways to be alone together so you have a chance to talk," he offered.

I felt defensive. "But I can't ask him out. It would be so awkward, and I don't want to push him if he's not ready."

"Andrea, my guess is that Aaron won't pursue you until he knows how you feel."

"Really?! That's so unfair!" As soon as I said it, I realized my hypocrisy. I didn't want to admit I had feelings for him until he showed that he had feelings for me. It seemed like an impossible stand off.

My dad had another thought. "Look, you're good at inviting him to do stuff, so keep inviting. If he doesn't want to be with you, he won't come."

His simple logic made sense to me, but it felt risky. I'd heard so often about women being too pushy and not giving men a chance to take the first step, that I worried I would be setting myself up for a relationship in which I had to take the initiative all of the time. I recalled advice I'd previously received from a woman I respected. Her husband seemed strong and quiet, and she was empathetic and outgoing, like me. She encouraged me to offer my relational abilities rather than holding them back and expecting a man to initiate everything. That advice led me back to her with a related question.

"Jill, how do I know if Aaron and I are a good fit?" I wondered.

She brought out a book and said, "Being different isn't all that bad, but you should be compatible in other ways. The author of this book says that compatibility is like money in the bank. When you have similarities or ways that you fit together, those are like deposits in a bank. Of course you'll be different in other ways, but if you have enough invested in the bank, you can afford those differences."

I went home and decided to take the free compatibility assessment from eHarmony. I'd never considered using a dating website to find a

UNFROZEN

spouse, but maybe they were on to something. I wondered what kinds of questions they asked. I was also curious if they thought anyone in their worldwide database would be compatible with me.

"We are sorry, but there are no matches for you at this time." I rolled my eyes at my computer screen and laughed. Of course there weren't. But maybe Aaron hadn't ever taken their test.

I decided to make my own compatibility list. I pulled out a yellow spiral notebook I had dedicated to writing about Aaron and turned to a fresh page.

OK. What do I think I want and need in a husband?

I started to list personality traits: "willing and able to make decisions, desire to learn, desire to change, stable presence, community minded, not controlling yet not intimidated by me, family man, willing to confront in relationships, not stuck in any mindset..." The list went on until I'd written over 100 qualities that were important to me in a husband. Then I went back through the list and started checking off the things I had already seen in Aaron. It felt strangely empowering.

OK. I don't know if Aaron's interested in me, but I'm not going to just wait around until I find out. First, I need to know if I'm interested in him.

The thirty miles between us made it difficult to come up with reasons to get together, so I decided to create an opportunity. There was no need to ruin our friendship. I would tackle this relationship puzzle with the logic and observational skills of a detective. But I didn't want to skip the hard stuff this time. If Aaron were the man for me, I wanted to struggle well. So I determined to be honest with myself and God about how I felt. I wouldn't press him, nor would I run away. I would meet this challenge with both logic and honest longing. I decided to follow my dad's advice.

I will keep inviting Aaron to this relationship as long as he keeps accepting the invitation. And, hopefully, I'll be able to determine if we are compatible along the way.

CHAPTER 15

The most logical place for me to get new glasses would have been my hometown eye doctor. But I was in an unusual circumstance that required a creativity defying normal logic. I needed to find a way to spend time alone with Aaron rather than relying on Brianne as a crutch. There was a department store with a vision center in Lexington where he lived, so I decided to get my glasses there.

Since I was teaching music again, I called him on my lunch break and left a message, hoping he would call back. With no guarantee that my plan would work out, I hopped in my car when school got out and headed toward Lexington.

If he doesn't call me back by the time I get there, I'll call him again. And if I don't get ahold of him, maybe I'll just go home and forget ordering glasses today.

My car rolled into the parking lot, and I turned off the ignition. *What if I called and he didn't want to…?*

My phone rang. Looked down, I realized it was Aaron and smiled.

Saved by the bell.

"Hello?"

It took a couple of seconds for Aaron to speak. "Hey. This is Aaron. I see that you called. So you need glasses, huh?"

"Yep." It was time to play it cool. "I'm headed in to order them now. I thought I should call since I'm in town."

"Do you want to come over when you're done?" he invited.

That had been amazingly easy. "Sure. I'll see you in a little bit!" Without being manipulative, I had just arranged the circumstances so that we had a chance to get together. It was such a relief that it worked out.

Arriving at his house, I was greeted at the door by Aaron and his little Jack Russell terrier. "George wants to go for a walk. Would you like to come?"

"Sounds good." His yellow house was on the outskirts of town, so we headed toward the country and found a gravel road, the Nebraska sky completely open around us. I prayed that our conversation would feel more balanced than my feet currently felt on the rocky path beneath me. We walked and talked for an hour before turning around. I wondered what his social life entailed besides his outings with Brianne and me.

"I used to be in a couples' Bible study when I was in med school. But, I don't like to spend too much time in singles' groups," he warned.

"Why's that?" I wondered if he felt that way about spending time with us.

"It seems like it's just a place to find a date."

Does he not want to date??

I wanted to be sure he was OK with Brianne and me calling him. "So how do you feel about hanging out with Brianne and me? I never know for sure if I should call."

"You can call me anytime." I breathed a sigh of relieved excitement.

He still wants me to invite him, so I will.

When it was time for me to pick up the glasses I had ordered, I let him know. We made plans to hang out that night. We didn't know where to eat, so he asked if I wanted to check out a little Italian restaurant in a town just down the road.

This definitely feels like a date.

We sat and visited around the fake flowers in our little rounded booth until our waiter placed our food in front of us. "Should we pray?" he asked.

I bowed my head and bit my lip as his words came out in little bursts, "God, thanks that we can spend time together...and please be with my patients and help them get better...and...be with Andrea's students... and thanks for this food... that we can eat Italian...Thanks a bunch. Amen."

A burst of laughter escaped like it had the night he took me to prom and told me about the dead guy in his living room. "What?!" he wanted to know.

"Oh, I've just never heard anyone thank God "a 'bunch' before." I wondered if God had been thanked a bunch by anyone other than Aaron in the previous 40 years. I choked back the leftover chuckles so I wouldn't embarrass him, but he didn't mind.

A few minutes into our meal, he got a phone call, and I focused on eating. A little annoyed that someone was intruding on our time together, I fumbled around with my food in agitation until my knife flew out of my hand, splattering tomato sauce all over my button-down, sea-green shirt. This time we both laughed. I went to the restroom and looked in the mirror at the stain.

It's nice being able to laugh at each other and not feel stupid or worry that he's offended.

As I took a wet towel to the splotch on my shirt, I realized that we were really comfortable together on a number of levels. *I can push up against him without knocking him down. I like that.*

Glancing into the mirror once more, I realized that my shirt was ruined. Oh well. I smiled. *He's worth it.*

A couple weeks later, I found myself wanting to talk to him about a book I was reading regarding church. Most of our conversations were about our families and work. I missed talking with others about theoretical ideas, and I wondered if he could fill that void for me.

He called, and I ended up spending most of the time explaining the concepts in the book. However, I couldn't put my thoughts together to take the conversation anywhere, and he didn't know what to say. Aaron seemed confused, and, after a while, he lost interest. Conversations like that one were the reason I didn't even consider him a possible match for me such a long time. Could we talk about everything that was going on in my head? The old feeling that I was "too much" for people crept back in.

Silly Andrea, talking circles around someone again about stuff he didn't even want to discuss.

Of course he didn't want to talk about the ideas floating in my head! Clearly, he was a doer, while I was a thinker. He seemed open to learning and growing in his faith, but he didn't have the same kind of interest in theology that I did.

I can't hide the fact that I care about theology and how it works out in real life. I have always thought about this stuff, and I always will. How could I expect him to ever catch up? Is that even necessary? It's not like I will ever catch up with his understanding of biology.

Aaron felt like such a great match for me on so many levels, but I wondered if I would drive him crazy with discussions like this: If we wound up being a couple, was it OK for me to know more about the Bible and theology than my husband did?

Aaron is passionate about health, in general. Maybe God is bringing us together to help us grow and balance each other out. If I respect the knowledge and passion God has given Aaron in these areas and I am open to how he might impact me, maybe it's OK that I am passionate and interested in other areas. Maybe our differences are good for one another.

The real question I needed to ask was, would we be willing to work through such differences in the way that we thought and acted? Could we balance one another out? Or would there be friction when Aaron talked about the discipline and responsibility of our health and silence when I brought up the concepts I wrestled with in my mind?

I went back to my compatibility list and thought about each of the times I checked new items off when I saw them in Aaron. There were so many, I couldn't imagine anyone else being more compatible with me, overall.

I really, REALLY value who Aaron is. Do I have to give it all up just because I'm a theory freak? Can two people who think so differently live together well? I've yet to meet someone with whom I can both have theoretical conversations and with whom I would also want to build a life together.

Had I been trying to find a husband just like me? I knew it wasn't possible, or even ideal. Real connection takes place over the shedding of blood, sweat and tears. It's not automatic. Had I been looking for some impossible ideal to form right away?

I'm willing to try if he is. I just wish I knew if he were interested in me beyond friendship. He acts like he's willing to play the game, but he holds his cards so close to his chest. I wonder, what is he thinking?

It was the middle of November, and I was growing weary of being the person initiating opportunities to engage in our friendship. But I invited Aaron to meet Brianne and me at a high school football playoff game.

He called on his way down. "I'm bringing Lara with me. She's a traveling physical therapist, working at our clinic. I thought she might like to have something to do tonight."

"OK, great. See you in a while. We'll save you seats." I hung up my phone and gawked at Brianne. "He's bringing another woman!!!!! I can't believe this!"

She looked shocked, then seemed to change her mind. "Oh, Andrea! You know Aaron. He's probably just being nice."

"I don't want him to be nice to another woman. I want him to be nice to ME!" I felt as dramatic as a high school girl, but I had cooled down by the time they arrived. I peeked at him from under my warm little black hat with the pink flower on its side and smiled. Every once in a while, my red coat sleeve brushed up against his arm. I wasn't sure when I'd flirted so much.

After the game, we decided to go out to eat. We found a rustic bar and grille and sat down. Before long, Brianne had Lara in a discussion on the other side of the red and white checkered tablecloth so Aaron and I had time to talk on our own.

Thank you, Brianne!

When the waitress came around, Aaron ordered a diet Mountain Dew and a salad. I looked at him, perplexed. Don't real men want to eat steaks or big juicy burgers after a football game? "Why did you order a *diet* Mountain Dew and a salad?" I laughed.

He looked at me, unfazed. "Diabetes."

"You have diabetes?!" I asked, concerned and confused. How did I not know this by now?

"No. I don't want to get diabetes," he shrugged.

I looked at all 140 pounds of the skinniest 26-year-old blue eyed blonde guy I'd ever met and laughed. "Really?! You don't look like you're anywhere close to getting diabetes." I'd never seen anyone take such drastic preventative measures when they had no indication that a diagnosis was just around the corner.

He was dead serious. "And I don't ever want it."

I wondered what he thought of the burger, fries and Coke headed my way. "So how are things in Lexington?" I decided to change the subject. We caught up on our work and families until he perked up with another thought.

"I got a call from my friend Jeff." I had met Jeff once at a wedding. He was a good friend of Aaron's from PT school. "He and his wife Tara are leading a mission trip to Peru in March. They're putting on sports camps for kids."

"Oh?" I could tell he wanted to say more. "So are you going with them?"

"I want to."

In a very dark corner of my mind, I thought about the fact that a mission trip in March would take a lot of his vacation days at the beginning of what, in my mind, could be a big year. I could think of other ways to use those days!

"So when's your spring break?" he asked.

I mumbled an answer, happy for him yet a little annoyed that he seemed so ready to spend his vacation elsewhere.

"Do you want to go to Peru?"

I pulled my head up and looked for his laugh. But Aaron wasn't joking.

Ahhhhhh! Are you KIDDING me?!?!?!?!

I was freaking out on the inside, but I played it cool on the outside and gave him my most spiritual and true answer. "I have actually been thinking about finding a mission trip for this summer."

"Well, this would count. Then you would be free this summer," he smiled.

CHAPTER 16

Waking up too early the next morning, I couldn't fall back to sleep. Aaron's suggestion that I go to Peru whirled in my mind. So I lay there for hours, thinking about Aaron and the entire situation.

If he wants me to come to Peru with them that much, then he really does like spending time with me and isn't ever trying to avoid me! In fact, I think he likes me! He really can take initiative when he decides to. I am so glad to know for sure that he has it in him.

Shock gripped me. There were so many thoughts floating in my head.

I can't help but think how perfect Aaron is for me. I mean, really. He is SUCH the man I have been looking for. Strong. Courageous. Compassionate. Motivated. Determined. Mature. Stubborn. Adventurous. And, dang it, the man isn't intimidated by me! I can't believe it!

After over three months of honestly and earnestly praying and thinking about our relationship with longing and logic, we had kept moving forward. Not too fast, not too slow.

Well, maybe I didn't always like the pace, but I felt more confident of each step we took forward than I'd ever experienced before. Each footprint left a deep impression, indicating that our forward momentum carried much weight. We weren't floating on the clouds; we were treading a path with intention and with our long-term goals in mind. That's how it seemed to me anyway.

The next day, my dad and I sang for a funeral. We sat in the balcony up and behind the congregation as they gathered below. I had a little time before the service started.

"So, Dad. You know that Aaron came to the football game the other night."

"Oh, yeah! How did that go? Did you guys have fun?"

I told him about Aaron's surprise guest, and he rolled his eyes a little and chuckled. "Then after the game we went out to eat, and he told me about a mission trip he wants to go on. And he invited me to come with him."

"Really?! Where is he going?" Dad was always good at showing interest.

"Peru."

It was a good thing we were in the balcony and not where anyone could see us because Dad threw his head back, closed his eyes and laughed before he got out: "So the guy can't ask you on a date but he can ask you to go halfway around the world with him?!"

Touché.

For the next month, I struggled with that very issue. Our contact was sparse around the holiday season, which had me questioning if any of it was real. I told him I wasn't sure about going to Peru, but it was really our relationship I wasn't sure of.

After extensive pondering, I realized that I had been pretending all the time by playing it cool. Maybe I seemed indifferent to him. Was I hiding? I had thought I'd stopped hiding my feelings a couple years before. I knew I couldn't hide if I wanted Aaron to know how I felt.

Maybe I didn't know how to share my heart. For all of my efforts to grow in my ability to be real and take personal risks, I was scared to death. On one hand, I felt resentful about the messages I'd heard regarding gender roles in relationships, but, on the other hand, I didn't have the guts to do it differently. I recalled the advice I'd received once from another woman I respected. She'd noted that I'm particularly good at organizing and connecting relationally. Why expect a man – or someone with totally different gifts – to carry the relational load? While relying on some code of gender-conduct in relationships was safe, it was a way for me to keep from taking risks and trusting God. She'd suggested that I instead offer my gift. That was a very different message than I'd heard before.

Why was it so difficult to be honest about my feelings? Maybe fear lingered that, like Shane, Aaron would find me out and then let me know I was crazy for thinking he liked me. Perhaps I didn't want to start dating and find out that he felt trapped like Thomas had. Or maybe it was because I didn't want get into a happy relationship with him and have it stripped away three months later, as with John.

Or what if I just cared about Aaron so much that I wanted to honor him by giving him time to decide what he felt? Because of the value I placed on our friendship, it frightened me to think of the hole that would be left if our relationship ended.

I wanted desperately to go to Peru with Aaron, but, as the weeks went on, I also realized that the trip was three whole months away. My feelings for Aaron had come so far in the previous five months, I was convinced that by March we would either be dating or no longer be friends. Continuing in a relationship with him if it weren't moving forward would simply be impossible because I cared about him too much. Besides, I was tired of coming up with excuses for us to get together, call or email.

Ultimately, I decided not to start fundraising for the mission trip until Aaron and I could talk about our relationship. Something had to change, but I needed perspective first.

My good friends Trisha and Joe were home for the holidays with their new baby Hannah. We made plans for Aaron to come to my parents' house the next night to meet them. I had a feeling this meeting would be much different than the one at their apartment with Thomas two years before.

Aaron arrived a few minutes before they did. He walked in the door with flushed cheeks. I noticed, and the disease spread to me. We both acted like it was hot in my parents' home. But the fact was, we were both flustered, knowing that he had come specifically to see my friends. I would have postponed the meeting until we were actually dating had I known that they would be around. But this was our only chance, so I'd acted on it. And he didn't seem to mind.

A few minutes later, Trisha, Joe and Hannah arrived, and we went down the stairs to my parents' basement. I sat with Trisha on the sofa. Joe settled into the love seat across from us, and Aaron took the recliner next to my side of the sofa. Aaron seemed oddly at ease. They were gently inquisitive, and Joe got him talking about physical therapy. It was fun to hear Aaron talk about his area of passion and expertise. My admiration for him swelled.

He knows a lot! I would love to see this guy in action.

"So what's your background with church?" Trisha inquired. It was a natural question for a pastor's wife to ask. I figured she was curious about what he believed because the choice of one's church usually indicated that. But his answer made it hard to pin him down. He let them know that he went to a different church every year of college and med school. That was news to me. It was so nice to have someone else draw out interesting bits of information from Aaron.

After a couple of hours, the discussion quieted down. "Well, I'd better get home. Work tomorrow." He stood up and walked by Trisha, who was holding her sleeping baby. Ever so gently, he stretched out his hand and touched the back of his finger to Hannah's forehead. The image was so precious that I wanted to run to my room and cry. I knew his tender side had the potential to melt me.

There were two seconds of silence when Trisha, Joe and I settled back into our places in my parent's basement after he left. Then Joe looked right at me and declared, "I think he's great!"

Trisha lit up and nodded in agreement. "He smiles a lot. I like that!"

I sighed and fell back into my seat, "I know!"

"He seems pleasant and steady, a good complement to you."

"What are you saying, Joe? That I'm unpleasant and unsteady?!" I quipped.

But they knew me well. Trisha was definitely what I would call pleasant and steady. She and I were a good complement to one another when we worked on projects and discussed relationships over the years. Joe was a lot like me, and I'd been looking for a man more like Trisha for a long time.

"But seriously, you know what he said about his church background. It's that uncertainty and lack of theological knowledge that made it difficult for me to even consider him as an option for so long. I really thought I needed someone who was even more sure of his beliefs than I am, just to survive," I admitted.

Joe enthusiastically disagreed. "Aaron is open and growing and soaking it all up. He's great! So what's the next step?"

"Well, I know I can't wait until after we go to Peru to find out if we are going to move this relationship forward. I am already going crazy thinking about it. We have to go one way or the other. And he is the only reason I would choose to go on this particular mission trip. Raising money for the trip seems premature until I know he wants to start dating. But I don't want to push him, so I just feel stuck."

Joe shook his head, unconvinced. "You should tell him how you feel."

"Really?" I was hoping he would validate my intent to wait on Aaron.

He looked right at me, "Open and honest communication."

They left me with a lot to consider. But mostly, they left me feeling loved. It was a relief to have these dear friends affirm what I was thinking, and it did my heart so much good to have people I respected take an active role in meeting Aaron, giving me thoughtful feedback and helping me process things. Though I pondered a lot on my own or out loud with other people, I rarely had anyone join me in the process with a curious and bold love. There was something unique about the interaction that night that left me feeling less alone.

Joe made me think. I didn't know if I wanted to initiate a conversation with Aaron about our relationship, but I did think I should be more open and honest about how I felt. He would probably be taken aback if I told him I cared for him more deeply than a friend. I wanted to find ways to share my heart with him without shocking or scaring him.

Maybe I needed to tell Aaron when he blessed me or when I thought he was sweet. It would seem that kind of openness would be more appropriate and beneficial at this point in our relationship. I preferred to build the conversation over time rather than spring it on him overnight. It seemed healthier. Or maybe safer. I also knew that I wanted to talk to him face-to-face rather than by email. I wanted to build intimacy, not create more of a wall between what must be written with great thought and what could be said and responded to in the moment.

Joe wanted to know what the next step was, but I knew. I called Aaron and told him that we needed to talk. A few days later, I got in my car and headed to Lexington.

CHAPTER 17

My little white Bonneville rolled down the interstate, powered by my determination. I was through waiting on Aaron. Our relationship could go no further. Six months before that night, I'd made a cognitive decision to consider my compatibility for Aaron. Three months later, I was all-in. I knew I wanted a relationship with him, and I was almost certain that it could lead to marriage. For months he had continuously accepted my invitation to participate in our friendship. Thus, there I was on January 6th, 2005, with one question left in my mind.

Does he have it in him to take this relationship to the next level?

Even though I was certain that he was also interested in me, did he understand that there was no track left for our little friendship train? It was time either to jump over a lane and keep going full-steam ahead or to break up the cars and go our separate ways.

Turning onto Independence Avenue where his yellow house made its home, I laughed. *Mr. Independence needs me. I just hope he realizes it.*

The old Bonneville parked in the driveway, and I walked up to his porch. I was still impressed that he earned the down payment on his first house by mowing lawns with his brothers since he was nine, Aaron worked hard to take care of it. The oak trim lining the floors and doorways was a product of the labor of his own hands the year before.

Everything about Aaron was intentional, even the maroon curtains he had bought to make the house feel like his own home. We might not have shared the same style, but we both preferred to trim the fat off of everything we did in life. I called it being intentionally purposeful. Aaron called it "no-fluff."

All of my bold determination turned into monosyllabic grunts as soon as he greeted me at the door. I was far from my usual bubbly self.

"Hey. How was the drive?"

"Good."

"Do you want to go grab supper?"

"Sure."

"Do you want me to drive or…?"

"I can drive."

Good. I got out a sentence. Maybe driving will help me get my grip back.

We drove to a local burger joint and ordered salads. I found the green and white checkered tablecloth mesmerizing. Aaron seemed to feel the same way about his watch. It was the least engaging conversation we'd ever had.

How am I ever going to get this out if he's in such a rush? I'll bring it up in the car. Then I won't have to look at him.

He glanced at his watch again, "Well, we'd better get going."

We got back into my car and continued with our meaningless chitchat. I didn't know if I were trembling because of the cold January air or the impending moment of truth.

I can do this. I will do it before I leave this car. I can do this!

When I pulled into Aaron's driveway, I parked but left the engine running. My hands gripped the steering wheel, and my eyes fixated on his garage door in a desperate effort to be strong.

"Do you want to come in?" he asked.

I spoke before I let go. "OK."

Every ounce of determined strength gathered for that moment slowly drained into the ground. I turned the key, utterly defeated.

I can't do this. I will stay for a few minutes and then get out of here. I can't do it.

Aaron opened the door to his house and let me in. My courage was completely depleted by the time I made it to his couch, ten feet from the door. Aaron went to the back door and slid it open. I heard George zip in.

"Hi, George. How's it going, buddy?" I heard Aaron in the kitchen, but I remained paralyzed. "Do you want to see George's tricks?" he called from the corner behind me, grabbing a few treats.

"Sure!" I mustered a high-pitched response to keep from sounding as checked-out as I felt. I wanted to bury my face in the couch and cry.

Aaron returned to the center of the little greeting room with his dog. "Sit."

George sat, his eyes focused on his master. Aaron waited a couple of seconds before tossing him a treat. "Good boy!"

"Bang!" He stuck his finger out, pointing it like a gun at George, who immediately lay down on his side, waiting for another treat.

"Good boy!"

He continued, "Roll over!"

"Dance!"

I wasn't sure how it could be, but I felt incredibly impressed with Aaron's love and attention to his dog, while feeling totally jealous of George at the same time.

Aaron's voice dropped for the grand finale. "Patience..." George's eyes followed his hand as he set the soft, salty goodness down a foot in front of him on the floor. Aaron stood up and smiled at me. He obviously was particularly proud of this trick. George sat and stared at his treat. His focus reminded me of superheroes who use their eyes to burn through obstacles in front of them. But George kept sitting, seeming to trust that Aaron would release him to his reward soon. He waited 3...4...5 seconds. 10...11...12....

"OK!" George broke his trance and scarfed down his treat. "Good boy!" Aaron's hand stroked his dog's back and then patted him on the spot on his side four times. He sat down on the floor in front of me and scooped George into his arms, twirling his silky little ears in his fingers.

He would be a great dad.

I couldn't let my mind go any further. "I should get going," I managed without tears. I knew I wouldn't be able to hold them off much longer.

"Well, before you go," Aaron released George from his lap and rested on his hands behind him. "We need to talk."

What did he just say?!

Shocked, I muttered, "Yes, we do."

Is he really doing this right now? After all this time...he's really doing this right now?!

"We seem to have a lot in common. It's been good to see our friendship grow, and now it seems like the next step would be to start dating. What do you think?"

I felt like I'd stepped into one of my dreams where the headstrong princess gets herself in a pickle and is rescued by the unlikely hero.

"Yes." I breathed a huge sigh of relief. "I can't go on like this."

Aaron went on for a few minutes, saying what he appreciated about our friendship and that he'd like to be more intentional about getting to know one another to see where our relationship might go.

I knew exactly where we were headed because my last question was finally answered. He totally had it in him.

CHAPTER 18

Holdrege basketball games were a family affair. A family member was coaching, and my parents were avid in their support. I was accustomed to walking into the game and tagging along with the family. Now walking in the door with Aaron the weekend after our talk, I felt validated as my own person. I wanted to wave my hands in the air and then point at Aaron.

That's right, people. I'm DATING this handsome man.

But I didn't have to. People noticed on their own. And people who knew us had something to say about it.

Aaron's dad "always thought that was a good idea."

His mom had always "wondered if it might happen."

Someone else thought, "It's about time you guys figured it out!"

A mutual friend professed, "Now, that's a match made in heaven!"

Aaron called us the A-Team, and our families were elated.

All of my old routines felt completely new. In the first weeks of dating, I had to remind myself that Aaron and I were finally more than friends. It was like walking through the same old hallway and noticing doors that had never been there before. My hand would stretch timidly toward a new handle, and I would peek through the window before turning the knob. But once the door unlatched, it would fling open to a completely new way of experiencing the world, Aaron by my side.

Aaron had a different way of describing the experience the night we watched the Super Bowl in my parents' basement. "It's interesting, because I didn't know you four weeks ago, and probably still don't know you too well now."

I pulled back, "What do you mean?"

Aaron tried to explain, "It just seems like I've learned a lot about you since we started dating, and I have a lot more to learn."

"Oh." I stared at the players bashing each other on the screen. His admission reminded me that I had spent more time than he had weighing all of the possibilities in the months before we started dating. I didn't like being ahead in that department.

Aaron noticed something was off. "Are you ok?"

"Yeah."

"Will this bother you later?" he wanted to know.

"Probably not," I wanted to sound pleasant, but I knew it was a lie.

"Well, I can tell you something that I knew I liked about you four weeks ago." Aaron seemed to be trying to make me feel better.

"What's that?"

"The way you care for your family and friends. I knew I hoped you would care for me like that too." His honesty was touching, and I certainly planned on caring for him like that. However, seeing past my own insecurity was difficult.

He appreciates what I do for other people? What if I mess up and I don't care for him like he hopes? Or he doesn't feel like I care for him well? Does he like me for what I can do for him, or does he appreciate the whole of who I am?

His words stuck with me the rest of the night, so I did what I could to hold myself together and refrain from thinking about it too much. He had no idea how I felt about those comments, but I pulled back and tried to stuff down my feelings, saving the tears for after he had left.

I couldn't shake the fact that I had always had major doubts that anyone would want me; the real me, I'd put an enormous amount of effort, time, thought, prayer and emotional energy into being sure of my own feelings for Aaron before we even started dating because I cared about him. So at this point, I couldn't help but feel like my feelings were deeper and more thought out than his. It was hard for me to feel like he saw me as anything more than a good opportunity rather than someone he truly wanted.

When he said he didn't really know me yet, everything I had ever felt was undesirable about myself, had hated about myself, and everything I knew I couldn't change about myself flooded my mind. I could just imagine Aaron realizing those things about me and then looking on me with disgust, distaste or boredom. I was convinced that the foundation of his feelings for me wasn't as strong as mine was for him, but I couldn't let that hinder our relationship. Maybe he would catch up.

We moved on and spent more time together, enjoying life as a couple. But in a dark corner of my mind, I couldn't shake my latent fear.

He doesn't know me. That must be the only reason he's still around.

I felt unsettled, insecure about our relationship. I wasn't worried about what he thought of me at that particular time, but I wondered what he would think of me when he saw all of the ugly things about me. It amazed me every time Aaron accepted another crazy aspect of who I was and chose to go on with us anyway. Still, I was scared that, one way or another, I'd lose Aaron. I worried that he didn't feel like he needed me as much as I needed him. I was afraid that the relief I felt about finding the right one was just a temporary tease. Most of all, I feared that I couldn't actually love and be loved fully.

You can't let fear get the upper hand, Andrea. Talk to him!

One evening I took a big breath and then admitted, "I've been struggling lately as I wonder about the future, and I want you to know. There is a significant part of me that is crying out to be rescued. Rescued from my job, my living situation, my feeling of worthlessness, my finances, and all the little details of life that you have under control. I know you're good at fixing things, and I guess I have been realizing lately that I'm hoping you'll fix everything for me. I know that's not right."

"I had a bad dream the other night," he stated.

What?! Is he totally ignoring my vulnerability here?!

"We were on a rickety, old, wooden bridge, and I leaned over to fix a bad board. I almost had it, and then I reached up to grab something, but I pushed you off instead."

"Oh my goodness! What do you think it meant?" I wasn't sure I wanted to know. The last time someone had a scary dream with me in it, he woke up with a panic attack and found relief only when he knew he didn't have to stay in a relationship with me. What was Aaron thinking?

"I guess I can't fix everything!" He laughed. "I know you want me to fix how you're feeling about the future, but I don't think I can. I just don't want to venture too much into the subject of the future until we've established the foundation for it. OK?"

"OK," I muttered.

He reiterated, "Just trust me."

His words were comforting for a moment, until I realized I felt like his dog George, staring at the desire of my heart while Aaron said, "Patience...."

Was he acting like my master and I his subject...his dog?! Was he the one in control and I the one waiting for him to release me to fully enjoy my reward? The thought infuriated me.

My insecurity continued to press in on my mind, despite the fact we were having so much fun dating. I reflected on my experience of our relationship by journaling every night before I went to bed, the good, bad and my own ugly.

I feel bad when I suggest that we do something and he doesn't want to do it. I would rather wait for him to suggest what to do so I won't have to be disappointed when he isn't excited about my ideas. When he rejects my ideas, it feels like he's rejecting me. This can't be healthy.

I'd had enough conversations with other girls to know I wasn't the only one who felt this way. My whole life I'd been reflecting on my own experiences to find answers – not just for myself, but for the world.

It's hard to be a girl in this situation! When I feel like men have control, I'm tempted to pull up my defenses, decide I know best, and then manipulate the situation to get what I want. I fight that temptation all the time. Either that or I bottle it all up because I feel foolish when he doesn't like my idea, and then I eventually explode when I can't take it anymore.

I wanted to find a better way for both of us, for all of us. It wasn't Aaron's fault for admitting what he did or didn't want to do. Perhaps he could have been more sensitive to my feelings, but he was in no way controlling. He was just honest. I knew this deep down, yet I still felt a little resentful.

How could I be so in tune to what he wants when he has no idea what I want? Maybe it would have helped had I just told him.

CHAPTER 19

In the middle of February, we spent the day together shopping for a Valentine's Day care package for my sister. Aaron's willingness to take such an interest in her was precious to me. Daniele lived on the East Coast, and he knew how important she was to me. We had even talked about the possibility of visiting her in the summer.

We went back to his house and sat down on the couch by the wood fireplace with the white stone hearth. I marveled again at the work he put into his home. It certainly wasn't feminine, nor was it my idea of a bachelor pad.

"So how are we doing?" Aaron asked. It was a familiar question, he'd been asking it periodically for weeks. It kept propelling us forward by giving us each the chance to reflect about where we'd been and what steps to take next. Some might call it excessive, but I called it a blessing. That day he called it our five-and-a-half-weeks assessment.

"I think we're doing pretty well." It was hard for me to know how much to say. I didn't want to go into all of my insecurities again. He addressed them well the first time, and we were having fun. "How about you?"

"I want to experience more of the day-to-day kinds of activities together. And larger family gatherings." I wondered if those were the next items in some checklist he'd made. It was nice to realize that he was putting intentional thought into building the foundation of our relationship.

We cuddled on the couch for a while in silence. We felt so close, but we hadn't yet kissed. It felt natural to be together, to relax my head on his chest while his hand stroked my hair. In moments like those, I wished there were no boundaries.

But both Aaron and I were committed to sexual purity until we got married. Neither one of us had gone that far before, and we had no intention of changing our standards when we were with each other. Our relationship was so precious to us; it deserved an even higher standard.

There was something special about waiting. At that point in my life, I looked back on all of my previous relationships, grateful that none of them were very physical. As easy and natural as it would've been to cross that boundary with Aaron, I had no intention of letting that happen. My mind and heart were set on following through with the commitment. He seemed equally resolute.

It was time for me to go. We stood up, and Aaron held me at my waist, resting his forehead against mine. He softly said, "You know what? I don't have a cold anymore." He had had a nasty cold for the past month, but I had realized his intention to keep me from catching it had caused him to keep his distance.

"I'm all healthy now. You know what that means?"

Uh...Yeah...!

But I said, "No."

"That means I can kiss you." And he closed the distance.

I thanked God for kissing and hugging, because there were times when words were so inadequate. Many times they wouldn't even come. I was glad I had made a list early on because, by that point, all the things I appreciated about Aaron ran together...so much so that the only way for me to express it all was to simply say from the depths of my heart, "I love you." But we hadn't said those words to one another yet. I hadn't said them to any man. So I could only write them in my notebook.

March arrived, and it was time for our mission trip to Peru. I thought back to November when Aaron had first invited me to come. I laughed at the thought of going on the trip if we'd still been "just friends" after all that time. It was true that I wouldn't have been able to stand it.

Our experience in Peru was eye opening and inspiring. We were there to help run sports camps for kids as a way for the mission to build relationships with the community. It was amazing to experience another culture together. I loved watching Aaron play with kids and find ways to serve others. He enjoyed watching me dive deep into transformational conversations with others on our team.

A week and a lifetime later, we returned to Nebraska with our team and headed to his house in Lexington where I had left my car.

"Do you want to go for a walk before you hit the road again?"

"Sure."

We bundled up, ready to walk out the front door, when Aaron reached over. "Wait," he pulled me close. "I missed your hugs this week." We'd kept our distance while on the trip so we could focus on our mission.

"I missed yours too." I leaned into his shoulder, amazed at how well we fit together.

"I knew going into this week that it would either pull us apart or draw us closer together." Aaron's voice held me as tightly as his arms did. "I am very glad that it pulled us much closer together."

Tears ran down my face and reached my silent lips. I couldn't speak. My whole being was wound up in his embrace.

"I don't know when you're supposed to say this, but I really do love you, Andrea. And I mean every little piece of it."

I pulled back and did something I hardly ever did. I looked him in the eye to give weight to my heartfelt words. "Me too. I love you, Aaron."

Our kiss was salty from the tears flowing down my face.

"You're so beautiful when you cry," he whispered.

He'd never called me beautiful before. It was amazing to me that he would not only be able to cope with the expression of my emotion, but he even found it beautiful. How could it be?

"I don't deserve this," he said.

My eyes met his as I recalled the years we'd been friends without thinking it could be anything else. "I don't understand how this happens."

"I agree. It's completely out of our hands."

I knew exactly what he meant. I didn't feel I'd done anything to deserve him or make a relationship happen. It just had.

We both knew it was time for me to leave. I waved goodbye and smiled, "That was the best walk we've ever taken!"

CHAPTER 20

Aaron seemed distracted the week before we were scheduled to leave for Washington, DC, to visit my sister, and I wondered if he were actually excited to make the trip with me. It was the end of May, almost five months since we had begun dating. But I felt like we'd hit a plateau in our relationship again for the past month. The next logical step was to get engaged, but I had no idea how long it would take for him to get there. We wouldn't discuss the possibility in detail or go shopping for rings weeks before he popped the question because I wanted to be surprised and he knew it.

One evening after a day in the city, Daniele took us to a restaurant claiming to be "The Friendliest Saloon in Town." We walked in, and I waited a moment for my eyes to adjust to the dark room. I wondered what was so friendly about a place so dimly lit.

But she led us through the darkness to the light at the back of the room. I drew in a quick breath as we poked our heads into the back half of the restaurant. A skylight ceiling let in rays of the setting sun, warming the green leaves gathered in vines and plants hanging around the room. Tiny white lights added to the magical effect. Bricks under our feet and on the walls hinted that this was a patio, but plastic green chairs around the tables and green and white-checkered tablecloths confirmed it.

"Wow! This is so cool!" I was enchanted.

The transition from the dark room into the patio felt quite a bit like what I'd experienced five months before when Aaron told me it was time to take our friendship to the next level. After so many years of dark confusion and struggle, Aaron was the warm sun on my soul, calling out my femininity, inviting me to stretch into a fullness I had never imagined possible.

The three of us visited while we ate. I excused myself to go to the restroom and returned to a decidedly bubbling Daniele. She gazed at me with wide eyes.

"What??" I wanted to know. "What did you tell him about me?!"

"Oh, nothing!" She changed the subject and asked for my camera.

"Why?"

"I just think you two need a picture here in this beautiful restaurant," she gestured to the space around her.

"Whatever you say, Daniele." I rolled my eyes before she snapped the picture. Aaron just chuckled.

Later that night at the Roosevelt Memorial, Daniele hung back as Aaron guided me through the granite walls and waterfalls. Then he asked a question I hadn't heard for a couple of months.

"So, how are we doing?"

Really? I can't imagine what other steps we could possibly take now.

I smiled. "I think we're doing really well, Aaron."

"I've been thinking that too. I really like your family and you seem to get along well with my family, too. We just seem to fit together." He sounded more tender than usual.

"I think so too." I was glad I could keep my thoughts to myself because they were beginning to sound frustrated.

There is nothing left to figure out, Aaron! This is romantic, but a little irritating. We can't move an INCH further down this path.

"Good." He turned me back around a corner toward a large waterfall. I saw Daniele peering at us, camera in hand, thirty feet away. Aaron steered me toward a granite block next to the four-tiered waterfall. Three roses and two glasses of champagne sat waiting for us. My inner dialogue rattled.

Is this....!?! No...surely not! Oh my goodness! This is HAPPENING!

Aaron pulled in front of me as we approached the roses and began, "The past few months have been amazing. I've loved getting to know you better..."

I could hardly take in his words as the enormity of the moment swept me over, much like the roar of water behind me. It was a good thing I could lean on him as he held me in his arms.

He reached down to the block of granite, picked up the red roses and handed them to me, one by one. "There are three roses here to represent our relationship. One for you. One for me. And one for Jesus. Because He has been in this from the beginning." Then he knelt down on one knee and asked, "Andrea, will you marry me?"

I couldn't stand being so far away from him, so my knees bent low as I declared, "Absolutely!" We kissed and held each other. I glanced over at my sister who was wiping her cheeks when she wasn't taking pictures.

"Good!" he sighed in relief.

Twenty-four hours later, we were back in Nebraska with a wedding date, a wedding party and an engagement ring. We would be married on September 24th, three and a half months later. It was just long enough to plan a big, hometown wedding, but not so far away that we would waste time before starting our life together.

We only had three months to prepare for our wedding, which for us also meant we had three months to prepare the yellow house on Independence Avenue for me. I wouldn't be moving in before we got married. Aaron and I saw our wedding as the beginning of our "'til-death-do-us-part" commitment. It was a momentous pledge, and we wanted our wedding ceremony to coincide with our physical union. It was our stake in the ground. Our pledge of good faith. Our weighty and disciplined promise. By then, we would be 27 years old.

It was hard to believe that it had taken us twelve years to figure out how well we fit together. Or maybe it had taken us that long to grow to a point where we did fit together. I recalled how appalled I felt toward the end of college when people had said, "You must not be ready to get married yet." The comment had driven me nuts back then. But as we prepared for our wedding, I wondered if there were some truth to that statement. I wasn't any less ready for marriage than the people in the dozen weddings I had sung for over the years, but maybe I wasn't ready for Aaron. For Aaron and me. For the kind of relationship we intended to form.

I had a strong sense of the hand of God on my life at that point. Much like the iconic poem about seeing one set of footprints in the sand, I often had felt like God left me in my moments of deep pain. But at this point, it was evident to me He'd been carrying me the whole time.

I thought about the relationships we'd each had in the past. One of my greatest fears through the years was that I would give pieces of my heart away that I couldn't retrieve and then give just a portion of it to my husband. The notion that I wouldn't be able to give my whole heart to my husband made me cringe. What did it all mean? Was I giving my husband less of my heart than he would have gotten had I not cared about anyone else along my path?

Now I answered that question with an emphatic "NO!" Closing my heart down during college and then opening it back up to grieve five years later had taught me that my heart was not a chocolate bar to be broken into pieces and consumed by others along my way. Rather, it was a distributor of love, and, as long as I was connected to the Source of love, I would never run out of love to give. Guarding it didn't mean I had to keep from loving others. It didn't mean that pain would cripple my ability to love fully for the rest of my life. I decided that guarding had more do with tending rather than blocking.

A gardener could hide her plants away from the wind, insects and scorching sun, but then they wouldn't be able to enjoy the rain and sunlight that make them grow. She could spray them with pesticides, but how would the food taste, and how could she know what side effect the chemicals might have in the future? She could pull every weed until her garden looked pristine, but how much time and energy would she have to share the fruit of her labor with anyone else? How much would she enjoy her garden?

The gardener who enjoys her garden and shares its abundance with others does not block it. She tends it. She plants and nourishes. She picks and prunes to make room for nourishment to grow. She watches the weather for signs that she needs to water twice that day or to provide cover to keep fruits and vegetables from being pummeled by hail. She tends her garden so that she can enjoy it and share it with others.

As I pondered what I'd learned about love, I felt grateful for the relationships of my past and all I had learned from them. My heart fully intact, I wrote a song called "Mercy Rain" and recorded it in a local studio so we could play it for our guests before the wedding. It served as a song of gratitude to God, our parents and those who had supported us along our journey toward one another.

A little boy, a little girl
Dreams and plans to conquer the world
Mercy.

Faith so young and hearts so unsure
A heritage of love that endures
Mercy.

And the prayers of those who love them
Dance in flight on up to the heavens.

Holy, holy One
Let Your kingdom come
And bless this precious life
O Lord be glorified.

The brave young man breaks forth on his own
With much to learn yet much to show
Mercy.

The woman jumps, not sure where she'll land
She reaches out but finds no hand
Mercy...

And the God of love shows His face
their hearts entwine, a gift of grace
Mercy...Oh, yes, mercy rain down.

Everything made sense on September 24, 2005. Every heartbreak, every shattered dream, made sense in light of what we found in one another. This wasn't a relationship we were testing out or using as a practice run. This was it. We were ready to start walking a new path, one of respect, love and honesty. It was our happily-ever-after.

SECTION FOUR:
RELEASING THE REAL ME

CHAPTER 21

Our wedding cake was heaven on earth. For me, eating the frosted delight was like tasting victory. It was so good that we packed a layer and took it with us to Estes Park where we honeymooned. We ate the sweet cake and then drank in the bliss of unity.

It was somewhat surreal to enter marriage with the knowledge that it would likely get really hard, quickly. I wished I'd had the courage to say out loud what I wrote to Aaron in my journal.

I really am quite insecure about us – not really about what you think of me now, but what you will think of me when you find out I'm not everything you want. I don't know what to do but gauge your reaction to know if I am annoying you or not.

A new doubt dogged me. Although I knew Aaron would never leave me, would he always love me, even if I messed up? I delighted him the day we got married, but what if I started to annoy him? Would he really like me then?

Unsure of the answers to those questions, I had no intention of leaving it to chance. We were happy, but I knew myself too well.

What will happen if I back the car into a big rock? How will he feel about me if I don't follow through on my daily responsibilities? What will he think of me if I gain weight? Will I be more trouble than I'm worth?

Those fears lurked under the surface of my interactions with Aaron. But I did my best to ignore them and be the best wife I could be. Loving him with all my heart, I was absolutely convinced that we were meant to be together. I'd done my research. Besides, I'd made my relationship mistakes. And against the odds, Aaron and I had made it past the seemingly impenetrable friendship-to-romantic-relationship barrier.

I knew I was more aware of how hard this was going to be than Aaron was. After all, I was the one with the counseling ministries degree. I determined let him down easy and make the honeymoon last as long as possible.

"Where do you want to eat?" Aaron asked. We hadn't eaten out much since the wedding.

I was in the mood for pizza. "How about the pizza place? We can have a big salad with our pizza," I winked.

Aaron grimaced. "I don't eat salad with pizza. It's like trying to fool myself into thinking I'm eating healthy when I'm not."

"Oh." I thought I'd found the perfect way to reconcile my desire for the occasional slice and Aaron's insistence on eating healthy. "How about the Italian place where we went on our first unofficial date? We haven't been back there since!"

"No. We don't want need to spend that much, and I need to get back home at a decent time tonight."

Apparently we had different ideas about what it meant to go on a date after getting married. I felt like I was failing my own test. Food wasn't worth sacrificing every ounce of respect my husband had for me, so I went with a different angle. "Where do you want to go?"

"Let's go to Subway. I'm in the mood for a salad."

The same scene played out a number of times during the first few months of our marriage until I felt like I always wanted the wrong thing. If I wanted something different than my husband did, I didn't tell him, and I convinced myself that it didn't matter. Where we ate or what we did for fun some nights seemed insignificant in the grand scheme of maintaining the honeymoon period as long as possible. I wanted to be desirable to my husband. Not just physically desirable, but desirable as a partner. I loved being on the A-team, and I wasn't going to give up our camaraderie by insisting on my preferences for food and simple activities.

The problem was that my attempt to please my husband above all else didn't end there. I started measuring my worth by how pleased he was with me. Subconsciously, I kept score in the back of my mind…

Healthy home cooked meal = +10 points. Late for a family gathering = -25 points. Iron his pants for work = +5 points. Healthy home cooked meal that isn't as healthy as I thought it was = -5 points.

Up and down my confidence went with each interaction. Hurt by the disapproving looks occasionally directed at me, I would explain, "I was busy trying to… so I forgot to…."

And then there were the times when I was oblivious to how what I said in front of other people could affect Aaron. On one occasion, his mood changed as soon as we climbed into our truck, and he shut his door.

Aaron fumed, "You just treated me like crap in there!"

"What?!" I didn't know what in the world he was talking about.

He found a few words to match his fury, "What am I supposed to do when you talk like that to me? I would NEVER do that to you in front of other people!" I'd never seen him so angry. Here I had been striving so hard to keep him happy with me, and I went and screwed it up with one word.

"I didn't know I did that. I just thought you…."

In spite of my lack of intentional disrespect, apparently he felt it.

Resentment started to set in underneath my apologies. *How dare he express his feelings when I've been working so hard to keep mine hidden?!*

I didn't tell him every time he made me feel small, so why did he have to make such a big deal about it when I accidentally did it to him? For goodness' sake, I loved him with all my heart, but he was making it sound like he would never recover from my mistake! I hated having that much power over him.

My internal posture toward Aaron became destructive. I so desperately wanted to trick Dr. Maier's "cycle of love" system and totally skip over the "I hate you" phase.

In order to project the image that I was the ideal wife for my husband, I needed to hide the flaws. Flaws, I was convinced, would make me ugly to him. When negative things slipped out of my "ideal wife" persona, I couldn't stuff them back in unnoticed anymore. He was right there. I didn't want to acknowledge that I had hurt him or had done something wrong because it would mean acknowledging the notion that I was less than he needed me to be.

I rationalized my actions and explained myself. He called it making excuses; I called it proving to him that I wasn't as bad as it seemed. I became sweetly defensive.

He saw right through me and didn't think it was sweet at all. "Why can't you just say that you're sorry?"

Conversation after conversation ended up in tension. I wanted to be beautiful in his eyes, and I needed him to respect me. After letting him have whatever he wanted, we still ended up with all of this tension between us! What more was I supposed to do? Bitterness invaded my heart, and I shoved it into a dark corner to avoid dealing with it.

The close physical and emotional proximity to one another made it difficult to keep from stepping on one another's toes and accidentally picking at each other's wounds. But it never felt like an accident. Every bump and scrape felt like an intentional effort to make the other feel horrible. We were hurt and confused. The pains of the past came up with great force. It was inevitable that we would touch each other's injuries; they were completely exposed.

It was hard to feel anything but betrayed when the one person I had trusted to make me feel better ended up making me feel worse. How had we ended up here so quickly, just months after our wedding?

My desire was to be beautiful to my husband and be the ideal wife forever, but my lack of honesty was creating barriers. I'd forgotten that I'd been in this situation before. Why was I trying to impress the one person who had promised to love me, no matter what?

Having prepared my heart for marriage, I had honestly thought that I had gone through so much internal brokenness and freedom when I was single so I wouldn't have to go through it after I got married. *How could I let this happen?*

CHAPTER 22

We made it through the first nine months of living and working together, and then we were off to Wisconsin. Aaron had been accepted into an elite sports physical therapy residency for the coming year, and we were thrilled to have a new adventure together. I was relieved to start a new phase of life on equal footing. We would be moving into our apartment, making our friends, and choosing our church together.

A few months later, I was pregnant and in a small group with other women tied to the residency program. At 28, I'd spent my adult years primarily with other single people, so befriending married women starting their families was a new experience for me. I admired their keen interest in knitting, quilting, gardening and cooking.

I wondered if being pregnant would flip the homemaker switch on inside me. Maybe I just needed to get used to being a woman who cares about the things these women cared about. Aaron would surely appreciate it, and I certainly wanted to create a haven for my family. So I took mental notes on how they took their shoes off at the door and held coffee dates in their intentionally decorated homes. I listened carefully as they talked of recipes using vegetables I'd never heard of before, like bok choy, kale and leeks. In spite of feeling like a fish out of water, I determined to grow feet and learn how to navigate this role of homemaker.

As my baby bump grew, I felt an increasing desire to imitate my friends so I could create a similarly homey atmosphere for my little family. So one day I went to the store and purchased knitting needles and yarn before heading over to my friend's house for my first knitting lesson.

The smell of decaffeinated coffee filled her home. "So you want to learn how to knit, huh?" She asked.

"I've learned a lot from watching you guys. I just haven't ever been very interested in cooking, decorating and crafts until now. I've always been focused on thinking about theology and relationships and that sort of thing. So I'm nervous about knitting because every time I've tried to do something that requires precision of hand, I mess it up."

"Oh, you'll do great. Knitting isn't hard at all. You might find it relaxing!" She encouraged in her gentle voice.

My friend went on to teach me the simplest knot and started me off on my very first knitting project.

It took a couple of weeks, but I was excited to see my scarf grow from the labor of my hands. I noted how much less guilty I felt for sitting and watching television when I had something to show for it. Aaron was off doing research and being grilled about all of the new information they were peppering him with all day, every day. The least I could do was knit something. Eventually, I completed the scarf and tied one last knot.

"I did it!" I remarked to my rounded belly. "Maybe I can make you a little blanket next!"

I held my triumph before me and blinked. Reaching down to pull the heavy end up from the floor, I realized that it was much wider than the end I had just finished. I placed the ends together and stared. One end was twelve inches long, and the other end was six! "How did I lose so many stitches?!" I looked at it and just started to laugh. My knitting project was just like all my other projects requiring precision of hand: a hot mess!

"This was supposed to be easy! Obviously, knitting isn't my thing. Sorry, little one, you're going to have to put up with a mom who doesn't craft." I immediately packed my needles and yarn and drove to my friend's house, laughing at myself the whole way.

She didn't know I was coming, so when she opened the door, I simply said, "Thank you for teaching me how to knit. I finished my scarf today, and it was horrible! I didn't enjoy it enough to get better at it, so I want to surrender these to you." I handed her my bag of needles and yarn.

Her eyes were wide with compassion, "I'm sure it's not that bad! You don't have to give up yet."

"I appreciate that, but I actually don't feel bad about myself. I just realized that I would rather get better at doing something that fits me better. But, seriously, thank you." If a woman in her third trimester ever bounced, I bounced down the stairs and into my car.

My knitting experience left me wondering what it meant for me to provide a comfortable home for my family. I knew I could provide great conversations, insights and encouragement, but could I provide a clean home, good food and an organized schedule?

And the more important question was, how would Aaron feel when I failed at executing the details of life? I wasn't sure. I only knew that I needed to find an Andrea-way to express my love and care for my family.

When it was finally time to have our first baby, I was ready and excited to jump into motherhood. Thirteen hours after being induced, we were thrilled to welcome our daughter Amelia into the world to the tune of Avalon's "Testify to Love."

Friends who worked in the hospital said that the nursing staff glowed with praise for Aaron and me. "Labor and Delivery is abuzz about this sweet couple that had their baby last night! They said you were the perfect patients. The perfect little family!"

We were pleased with how we'd made it through. Mistakes by nurses and doctors felt like small bumps in the road that we had managed with grace. I felt fabulous after giving birth. I hadn't realized how crummy I had felt as a pregnant woman until I was no longer pregnant.

But Amelia was jaundiced. They sent us home with a bili-blanket, a small pad with an ultraviolet light we placed on her back. Aaron called her his little glow-bug. Unfortunately, the take-home remedy didn't work, and Amelia had to go back to the hospital until her levels were normal.

I stayed in the room with her and had my first real experience of mommy shame. The nurse stuck Velcro patches on our baby's temples and gently covered her eyes with a special cloth to block the rays as she slept in a NICU bed under what looked to me like tanning bed lights. Aaron went home for the evening, and I settled into the recliner next to Amelia.

The doctor gently explained the situation. "We want to know how much milk your baby is getting. If she's not getting enough, we will need to supplement with formula so her body can flush out the bilirubin."

"How can you know that?" I wondered.

She glanced down at the breast pump on the floor. "That's why we had you bring the breast pump. We'll give you a few minutes to pump and that will give us an indication of what Amelia's eating."

The doctor left, and I looked around. The room was no larger than a ten-foot square with a crib and guest chair, besides the spaces Amelia and I already occupied. I'd never pumped milk before, but I'd heard of women doing it all the time. I looked at the instructions, removed my shirt and slipped the pieces in place.

I can do this. No big deal. I'm a mom, and moms pump milk for their babies.

I flicked the machine on and immediately felt as though someone had grabbed my breasts with a rubber glove, twisted, and pulled. "GUSHgush-GUSHgush-GUSHgush…" the machine sounded. I let out a little sob and wondered how long it would take.

Drip…drip…every few seconds a small drop of milk landed in each bottle. The door opened, and a male hospital worker started to walk in. I let out a little gasp and turned. As soon as he realized what he had done, he apologized and left. Humiliated, I covered myself with a blanket and cried softly as the pump continued to run.

Finally, no more drips fell into the bottles. The doctor came back. "It looks like you've got a little less than two ounces there. I recommend that we supplement with formula so you only have to stay overnight one night."

"OK." I was crushed. My first important task as a mom, and I was failing already. I couldn't knit, and I couldn't nourish. If this baby wanted to talk about the meaning of life, I would be the perfect mom for her. But babies don't wrestle with existential questions, so everything that could make me a good mom was wasted in her moment of need. I felt like a worthless cow.

Aaron came to sit with me the next day. He explained the situation to my parents with medical professionalism when they arrived. "Amelia's body just needs to flush out the bilirubin. The doctor said after one more milking, they'll test her again, and she should be ready to go."

Mom and Dad stared at Aaron as his word choice hit them, "Milking?!" I looked at them and started to giggle. Dad threw his head back, squinted his eyes and heaved. His laughter turned his face red. Mom took off her glasses and wiped the tears from her eyes. Aaron's face turned red as he looked at me and apologized, "I'm sorry! I mean…after she eats again…."

We laughed so hard that we cried! Aaron's little slip of the tongue brought welcome relief from the pressure to give my child what she needed.

It also reminded me that my husband wasn't perfect either. Maybe we could laugh at our imperfections rather than feeling threatened by them.

CHAPTER 23

In the hospital I realized that my gift of empathy had turned into the direct mirroring of the emotions my baby girl expressed. When they poked my daughter, I felt as though I were being poked. When she screamed, I wanted to scream, too. I continued to experience her feelings intensely once we got home, and it didn't seem to let up. At one point when Amelia was screaming, I told my husband, "I hear her cry, and I just start to cry along with her!" He didn't seem to have that problem.

But my empathy was not all bad. Amelia was engaging, had a beautiful smile, and I felt her pleasure as she giggled and cooed. For better or worse, I was intimately connected to our little baby girl.

I enjoyed my new role as a young mom. It was fun having a little buddy to accompany me on errands. We visited a nearby nursing home every Thursday to put smiles on the faces of residents. It was fun to share our daughter's sweetness with others.

But after a couple of weeks, she began to cry or even scream when I tried to feed her or put her to bed. I couldn't seem to anticipate her needs soon enough. Sometimes the screams would seem to come out of nowhere.

One night I took her to small group with the women whose homemaking abilities I admired. I walked in the door, hefting my sweet baby in her car seat. There were two other women in the group who had just had babies as well. We all swooned over their cuteness, then sat down to talk like grown-ups. I was ready to have some adult conversation!

Thinking that Amelia would go to sleep in her car seat, I covered it with a quilt one of my friends in the group had made for her. But a few minutes into our discussion, Amelia started to cry. Loudly. I pulled the blanket back to see her round little face turn red as she began to scream.

"Is she hungry?" someone asked.

"Oh, no. I just fed her before coming. I'm sure she just needs her binky." I searched for the pacifier and found it next to her tiny waist. She didn't take it right away, but when I gently rubbed it on the roof of her mouth, she began sucking.

"It's hard to know exactly what she needs. I keep thinking she's just fine, and then, out of nowhere, she starts to cry." The pacifier quieted her for a moment as she moved it around her mouth with her tongue, her eyelids shut and skeptical. Out came the pacifier and along with it, a hearty scream.

My heart started pounding, and my lips started explaining loud enough so everyone could hear, "She does this at night. You know, just starts screaming with no warning."

I gently unbuckled her from the car seat, pulled her close and stood up. "Sometimes she just needs to bounce."

Everyone was looking at me. I could see the empathy in their eyes, but I wondered what they were thinking.

"Maybe she really does just need to eat." I sat down again and prepared to nurse. I lifted my baby to my breast, but she wouldn't eat. She seemed to be angry that I didn't understand what she wanted. "I've been feeding her every hour and a half. I wonder if I'm just not giving her enough."

I looked down at Amelia and realized my body was hard with tension. There was no way milk would come out of there.

Are they feeling sorry for me because I have a baby I can't calm down? Do they think I'm screwing her up somehow? Maybe I am.

Amelia's screaming escalated. "Excuse me. Sorry, guys." I walked out of the living room and closed myself and my screaming baby into a bedroom. My ears hurt like someone was sticking needles in to my eardrums.

She continued to protest, though I knew not over what. "What is wrong, sweet thing?! Are you hungry? Are you tired? What do you want?!" I laid her wailing body down on the floor, stroked her cheek and started to cry.

I should know what my baby needs. I am her mom! What's wrong with me? What's wrong with her?...How could I blame her? She's just an infant!

Someone knocked on the door and came in. "Can I do anything to help?"

I hid my face so she couldn't see my tears. "No. We just need to go. I'm sorry we've been so disruptive."

"You don't need to apologize," she offered.

I picked Amelia up and went back into the living room. "Sorry, guys. I guess we need to go."

The women in the room sat on the edge of their seats, concern in their eyes.

"It's OK."

"We all understand."

"We'll see you next time."

"I'll grab your stuff," the hostess offered.

Tears ran down my face as I bustled out the door, my baby in my arms. We got to the truck, and my friend helped me get the car seat set in the cradle correctly. Amelia was still screaming.

"It's a good thing she's so cute!" my dear friend said as she gave me a hug.

I thanked her for her help, maneuvered my tense body into the driver's seat and took off. Amelia and I echoed one another's cries the whole way home.

When she wasn't upset, our little baby was a delight. Aaron got home late every night from a long day stretching his skills, teaching PT and athletic training students, or answering the high pressure quizzes over his shoulder from his mentors. I wanted to be sure to let Amelia bless her daddy with her sweetness; so, every night around eight, we would greet him with smiles.

However, most nights around 8:30, a switch flipped in our daughter. One moment she would coo at us, and the next she would scream as though we were hurting her. We were sure our neighboring resident would call the police. But one night we finally found a way to quiet her.

"Let's try the heartbeat music," Aaron suggested.

"I've tried it before, but I don't think she can hear it over her own screams," I answered loudly enough for him to hear. We brought her into our room and started the rapid heartbeat sounds on the CD player. "Turn it up," I suggested.

Aaron turned it up, and I brought Amelia's ear close to the speaker, held her close to my chest and bounced up and down. The switch flipped again. Amelia stopped screaming and opened her eyes. Aaron and I looked at each other and smiled. I stopped bouncing our little bundle of joy, and she wailed again.

"I can't hold her all night," I spoke through tears of exhaustion. Aaron grabbed her blanket, and we swaddled her arms close to her sides, then wrapped her in the thick baby quilt my friend made for her. Amelia's screams were escalating again.

"You try!" I gave the bundle of blankets to Aaron, and he took her back to the speaker and began bouncing her close to his chest again. She immediately stopped crying, but we knew that wasn't enough. Aaron continued to bounce her for a few more minutes until her eyes closed and her head tilted to the side.

He looked at me and raised his eyebrows. I nodded over to the bassinet, and he gently laid her down. We tiptoed backward out the room and shut the door, the heartbeat sounds still playing on the cd.

I grabbed my husband and pulled him close. "Good job, honey."

He smiled and kissed my forehead, "Good job."

We moved when Amelia was three months old, and Aaron completed his residency. There were a number of exciting and troubling events that kept us on our toes as we settled into a new community and life closer to our families. Amelia's temperament calmed slightly as she moved from newborn to the baby stage, and we became quicker to recognize when our baby might become overwhelmed. We played heartbeat music every night, all night, to help all of us sleep.

We were glad to be back in Nebraska with our families, but when the newness of the move wore off and the stress mounted, Aaron and I found ourselves unintentionally picking at each other's wounds again.

Little disagreements felt like catastrophic contention. Accidental offenses felt like intentional attacks. We always made up after offending one another, but sometimes it took days to cover the emotional distance between us.

I was excited to have found a bit of stability in Nebraska again. It was the first time since I had let go of the ideal self that broke down in seminary that I could settle in and look for opportunities to offer myself to others.

I rekindled a mentoring friendship with a college student, and soon our one-on-one coffee dates turned into a small group gathering. The group of college women grew, and we claimed the name Uprising. Aaron and I hosted gatherings over the course of three years with 12-25 young women huddled in our small basement, while Amelia slept upstairs with a fan running like a plane engine to kept her asleep.

I was relieved to find a purpose outside of feeding, diapering and quieting my baby. Amelia may not have been wrestling with inner turmoil, but these liberal arts college women certainly were. This, I could do!

Uprising was characterized by food, Bible study and authentic sharing. We made it a point to have a box of tissues handy all of the time because we often needed them. Our love and respect for one another grew, and yet our interactions were mostly limited to Thursday nights from 7-11.

After a year together, one girl noted to the group, "I know all of your deepest feelings and thoughts, but I don't know your majors or where you live!" Deep discussion and caring interaction were exactly what I wanted out of relationships, so it was exactly the kind of culture I cultivated in Uprising.

We held a retreat each year, the first of which we entitled "The Real Me." With 80 college women and mentors in attendance, I cast a vision of knowing and sharing our real selves with ourselves, God and others. At one point I read from Genesis 3, after Adam and Eve had disobeyed God and hid from Him in the garden. Rather than portraying a punishing tone, I read it as though God were sad. The girls leaned in as I read

God's question to Adam and Eve as a loving invitation:

> "'Where are you?' God asks. Perhaps God was not only giving Adam and Eve a chance to come out from physical hiding, but also from hiding their perceived internal ugly, sinful or weak parts of themselves so they could see that they actually needed God. Perhaps God wants to demonstrate His love for us, no matter what we've done. Perhaps we can trust Him with the truth deep inside. Because God doesn't gloss over how we mess up and tell us 'it's OK.' He allows us to feel the weight of wrongdoing, the gap between our weakness and His strength, and He tells us, 'You are forgiven. You are loved. I will be the strength in your weakness.' Are you hiding the real you from God? You don't have to fix yourself up before coming to God. He wants you, just as you are. The real you."

I noticed tears streaming down the face of a usually bubbly freshman. She cornered me later to let me know that she had never considered that God might be sad about Adam and Eve disobeying Him. "I always thought God was just angry all of the time. He really loves me?!" she marveled with tears in her eyes. Her enthusiasm and wonder gave me goose bumps and I felt great longing – a call to proclaim this beautiful news to the world.

The last morning of the retreat, I sat down on a chair in front of the whole group and read the prose and poetry I had written the night before.

> "Calling? Screaming is more like it. I have never in all my life felt so passionate and convinced that I could be made for a purpose. Not that I wasn't made for anything else – loving my husband and daughter well trumps all other callings in life. But right now, in this moment, I feel that turning my back on, neglecting, or even pursuing with less passion, this call would be flat-out disobedient. By the grace of God, I am what I am. By the grace of God, I am no longer stuck in a binding mode of self-preservation. I fail, but it's not my constant state. I am defensive, but I can let down my guard. I want to be strong,

but I realize that my strength is in what I used to perceive as weakness. God's grace brought me to this place."

I looked out at the young women sitting on the floor, leaning in as I continued to expose my heart. Maybe this was what it felt like to let myself go like the people at the poetry slam in The Green Mill had.

"And now by the grace of God, I am learning about the Gospel of Jesus Christ from a fresh perspective. My theology isn't new. My orthopraxy isn't new. The idea that the current Christian culture could shift isn't even new. But the way I look at Jesus is. He's so much more than my salvation for the afterlife. He's so much more than a member of the Trinity. He is life. Knowing him is eternal life. It's life to be tasted now and in community. It's….

It's earth.
Walking in a gentle rain,
Picking apples from my neighbor's tree,
Plodding up a 14'er and taking in the endless landscape
of snow-packed peaks,
Descending into a bed of flowers,
It's love.
Crying with someone who mourns,
Screeching for joy with someone who celebrates,
Rolling around the bed with my husband and sharing a blizzard,
Stroking my baby's bare cheek and tickling her tummy,
It's spirit.
A stirring in my soul that beckons me to action,
Trusting in a Father whose compassion is greater than my heartache,
Quiet,
It's passion.
Singing my heart out in the car,
Crying to "In My Arms" every time I hear it,
Trembling with conviction as I say, "I love you,"
Proclaiming good news of grace and freedom.

It's victory
Over addictions,
Over self-preservation,
Over hatred,
Over ignorance,
Over death,
It's life."

I counted it a great privilege to call these young women out of fear and shame and into the light of God's love for them! We all left the retreat on a high, feeling connected to God and one another.

But as Uprising met through the next year, I found that inviting people to be real carried with it a great weight, because real is messy. I decided that I needed to be prepared for incredibly difficult conversations, so I made a little internal promise to those women, that I kept to myself in my journal.

You cannot surprise me. I will not be shocked if you confess a struggle or hurtful action. I will not be shocked if you admit to lying or cheating. I will not condone actions I don't agree with, but I will not shame you into changing. Because I don't believe people really change when they do it under the threat of shame. I will, instead, use the most compelling form of invitation I know: love. I will be with and for you.

For the most part, I think I kept my secret promise throughout my time with Uprising. But it became more complicated. More difficult. More messy. I was pregnant again, and, as my own well-being deteriorated, Uprising changed.

CHAPTER 24

Halfway through our second pregnancy, I was incredibly uncomfortable. My inability to handle the emotional and physical demands of daily life started to overwhelm me. The pressure on my body and the needs of a 1 ½ year old were wearing on me. Emotionally overburdened, I questioned if I had the strength to endure everything.

It's likely I became depressed in the last part of my pregnancy. Even under normal circumstances, I didn't handle pain well, so with the additional constant state of demand on my body, fatigue and the general pressures of life, I struggled enormously. Aaron wasn't doing much better. It all set us up for the perfect storm in the delivery room.

We decided to try to give birth naturally, without medication. Labor with our first child had taken thirteen hours, so, when we went into the hospital around 5:00 p.m., we thought we would be at it all night. I settled into the whirlpool, and Aaron settled into the Laker's game. But before I knew it, my contractions were coming hard and frequently. Their intensity frightened me.

Oh boy! This is bad. Really bad. If I don't get that epidural soon, this is going to be unbearable.

I needed to share my urgent concern with my husband so he could get the anesthesiologist for me: "Aaron....AARON!" I felt bad about disturbing his playoff game, but..."I need the epidural."

He stood in the doorway and stared at me. I was aware that it generally took him a while to process new information. He was an expert at thinking things through to be sure he was making the right decision before taking action. He liked to be prepared. I loved that about my husband, just not in that moment.

"I need medication FAST!" Nearly shouting at him to break his trance, I tried to snap him out of his shock that I was changing our plan. "Go get the nurse, and tell her I want the epidural!"

"I thought..." he tried to say. But I interrupted him. "I CHANGED MY MIND!!!! Hurry!!!"

He left, and I made it out of the whirlpool and onto the toilet so I could "take care of business" before things really got going. In spite of feeling a little concerned about the way I had just spoken to Aaron, I was WAY more concerned that I get myself ready for what was coming.

Then a nurse walked in. "What are you doing?!"

Wasn't it obvious? I had a notion to ask her the same question! I covered myself as best I could and wondered, how it was OK for a stranger to walk in on me during such a vulnerable moment?

"You can't do that," she said.

I shook my head slightly at the impertinent comment. "I just need to go to the bathroom real quick." Grimacing as another contraction squeezed my abdomen, I threw my head back, moaning over intense pressure on my back.

"Having a baby feels like going to the bathroom. You need to get out here to the bed so we can check your progress." She walked over and put her arm around me to help me up.

But it didn't feel like help. It felt like I was living out a recurring nightmare I'd had in which I walked out onto a stage naked, completely unprepared for my concert. Except here, in real life, I was being dragged onstage instead of choosing it for myself.

"No! I really do need to go to the bathroom real quick, and then I'll come out!"

Is she pulling me now? Am I pulling back?

With difficulty, I managed to wrap myself up just enough to avoid feeling completely bare and to cover the waste I was sure must be leaking out of my body. Aaron and another nurse were waiting in the room to help me onto the bed. Embarrassed at how I must appear to them, I refused to look at anyone .

Turning my body so they wouldn't see my backside, I was climbing onto the bed when another contraction hit. I writhed and wailed as the intensity of the pain inside of me collided with my shame over the humiliating position I felt the nurse had put me in. At last I made it up onto the bed, continuing to evade eye contact.

In between breaths, I forced a nearly whispered question, "How soon can the epidural come? Please tell him to hurry!" Someone checked my progress, and I wondered if they also had to clean up after me. The thought horrified me.

Within minutes, the contractions came in waves, one right after the other. Why it was taking so long for the epidural to come?

The bed was elevated in a nearly seated position, with me on my side. My hands clung to the top of the mattress while my head flailed back and forth. At one point, on the low end of a contraction, right before another one started up again, someone came up to me with a clipboard and a pen. "What's this for?!"

"I need you to sign for the epidural."

I strained my head so I could see the woman's face. She had to be kidding! I knew there was no way I could hold still long enough for someone to stick a huge needle into my back without paralyzing me.

She continued to stand there through another contraction, so I went ahead and signed the paper. Not only was I ripped from the bathroom, now they were patronizing me. I didn't have long to think about it before a new wave of pain swept over me.

"Aaron!" He was standing on the front side of me. "Come push on my back! Please!" I knew I was experiencing back labor as I had with Amelia. His fists in my lower back had helped last time; maybe it would help this time too. "Harder! Harder!" It was no use. Nothing helped.

"I can't do this!" I tried to tell everyone in the room. "I can't! I can't do this!"

"Oh God, am I going to die?" I could hardly breathe.

"I want to die, God. Just let me quit! I can't do this! I'm trapped!"

I strained my body any way possible to relieve the pain. *I'm stuck! Why won't someone help me?*

"Jesus! Help me!" I cried out loud.

Aaron leaned over my back and toward my ear. "Shhhhhh! Shhhhhh!"

In that moment, I ripped my heart out of his hands and barricaded it back in my chest. No one would numb my physical pain, but nothing could force me to feel the emotional pain of losing my husband's respect.

In the middle of the emotional and physical turmoil of that moment, Aaron's simple attempt to help me calm down felt like death. Now, not only had I lost total control over my body and my situation...not only were they all patronizing me by making me think there was a chance my pain would be relieved...not only did I literally wish I could die to stop the pain...but also my husband, whom I respected more than anyone in the world, was embarrassed by me.

I had nothing left to give. Yet my body kept taking it from me.

No one would save me. I felt like I was completely at the mercy of God and everyone around me. And yet, where was God while pain ripped through my body and tore me apart from the inside? Where the hell did He go?!

Part of the reason I had wanted to try to deliver without medication in the first place was that I had heard that the mom and baby feel more connected immediately after delivery because they aren't numb from medication. I had also wanted to see if I had it in me to do what countless women had done since creation. But when I pushed for the last time and Grant entered the world, I was in shock. Regardless of what I should feel, I couldn't feel anything.

The doctor, who only saw the normal end of the delivery, told me: "You did a great job!"

Lying frozen in my awkward position, unable to respond as he stitched me up, I wished someone would tell him that I needed pain medication because I was unable to talk. Like an electric shock, each prick of the needle only added to my torture.

Finally, I muttered a request for medicine. The doctor hadn't realized I hadn't had any at all. He noted the large bruise on Grant's little arm, "No wonder it was painful; his elbow and your back must have had quite the fight during delivery."

After completing the usual paternal duties, Aaron sat down in the corner of the room, exhausted. I looked over at him, but I didn't see joy on his face. His eyebrows came together ever so slightly, and he shook his head. Turning away, I didn't look at him again for months.

Grant was born about 11:45 p.m., and we got to our room after 1:00. All night long, I lay in bed awake, shivering in shock, feeling like I'd lost it all. I'd lost my voice, any sense of control, my own self-respect for having wished I could have died; and, worst of all, I was convinced I'd lost the respect of my husband. Without any sense of respect, I was a shell of the woman I had been.

Assuming that Aaron was embarrassed that I'd been out of control during labor, I had no energy to consider any other possibility. My voice was trapped inside, and I had no idea how to let it out. I certainly couldn't ask him about it. Unable to sleep, I shuddered over my memories of labor, hyper-aware of my husband's disdain, even as he slept on the floor beside me.

I told no one. For all they knew, I was a proud mom of a new baby boy.

I shivered in the dark. *Just stay away.*

CHAPTER 25

A couple of days later, a nurse came in to give me instructions. The responsibility of heading home with a newborn weighed on me. While I didn't want to stay in the hospital any longer, I didn't want to go home and coexist with a husband who didn't respect me either.

This nurse was gruff, and I didn't have the strength to handle her insensitivity. In the middle of her matter-of-fact discourse, I couldn't stop the tears that escaped like fugitives down my cheeks. "Oh, honey, are you depressed?"

"No," I snapped, "I am a counselor." It was a half-truth, but I needed her to leave me alone. "I would know if I were depressed."

"Oh. OK. Well, you be sure to tell someone if you're depressed," she said before wrapping up her instructions.

It irritated me that she would suggest such a thing. People aren't necessarily depressed just because they cry. I had just had a baby! What did she expect?!

No amount of prior education or counseling experience could get me out of my predicament. However, making myself vulnerable to the medical staff again was not an option.

After she left, I convinced myself I would be fine. My body just needed a little rest and time to recover. Then I wouldn't be trapped anymore. I would just take care of myself since I certainly couldn't trust anyone else to care for me.

Although my harshness with the nurse bothered me, I couldn't be real with her. I couldn't be real with anyone because all I really wanted to do was cry all of the time. With an infant and a two-year-old, I couldn't do that. And though I loved my husband, I was scared to death of his disapproval. Mustering up just enough pleasantness to get through my interactions with him, I then ignored Aaron as much as possible.

When it was time to dress Grant and take him home, Aaron came into the room. Hyper-aware of his presence, my defenses went on high-alert immediately. Fearing that I would see his disappointment with me if I looked at him, I simply didn't.

"Please hand me his diaper," I said coldly.

"Here."

"Thanks."

I changed Grant's diaper, and Aaron reached in to help with his clothes.

My arms tightened like a bow drawn back with an arrow. "I've got it."

"OK. Is something wrong?"

"No." It irritated me that he would reach toward me without seeing what I really needed. "Would you please get the car seat?"

Surely things would get better when we went home if I just didn't talk about it. Maybe we just needed to get out of the hospital. But I remained outwardly tense to protect my internal fragility.

Aaron tried a couple of times to ask me how I was, but I could hardly speak, let alone put into words, the shame I carried with me.

Whenever I had to be around people, I tried to numb my feelings in an attempt to forget how terrified I felt. Even though I avoided thinking about my time in the hospital when I felt helpless and invisible, inevitably one thing or another would catch me off guard. The pain and embarrassment of giving birth would rush back over me.

My mind and body's natural inclination was to cave in on itself when this would happen. Although I couldn't always curl up in a fetal position to protect myself from the outside world, I wanted to. Nothing I did could fend off the heartache.

Mom stayed with us for a week as we adjusted to life with two little kids. She cooked, cleaned, played with Amelia and held Grant whenever I needed a break. She also served as a buffer between Aaron and me. If we had an audience, I didn't have to speak intimately with him.

When Grant was a week old, a friend brought over supper in a fun, blue gift bag. We ate up the pulled pork sandwiches, oriental salad, grapes and brownies like it was a feast! She thought of everything, including blue plates, napkins and cups. She even tied soft blue ribbon around the napkins and blue plastic ware. Then, like a Trojan horse, the attentive and loving gesture reminded me how un-cared for I'd felt in the hospital.

Pulling back from the table so I could lean over my lap, I confessed to my mom in the presence of my husband: "I don't think everything is right with me." I didn't expect him to understand or do anything to help me.

Mom turned her attention from Amelia picking at her plate and toward me. "It's hard having a baby, and you know your hormones are still trying to settle down."

I almost didn't say anything else, but the urge to leave the table was so strong I wanted them to know. "No. It's more than that. Right now I want to just curl up in a fetal position and cry. I feel like that every time I think about the hospital."

Mom's eyebrows moved toward one another in concern. "Oh, Andrea.

No, that's not normal. You need to tell your doctor about that."

"I think I need to ask Espen. I'll email him tonight." I didn't really need permission to email my friend's husband who was a psychologist, but it felt better to let Aaron know, even if I'd effectively shut him out of the conversation.

That evening I researched the symptoms of PTSD online, I wondering if something about labor and delivery had been traumatic for me. I certainly felt like it was, but what had happened to me that didn't happen to every other mother who gave birth naturally? Why would it affect me like that while I had friends giving birth at home like superheroes?

I emailed my friend Chris and her husband Espen with whom I consulted whenever I came upon a counseling situation that warranted his advice. This time I needed it for myself. After hearing the description of my symptoms and experience with labor and delivery, he suggested that I might have had a panic attack in labor. That would explain why I felt out of control and like I might die. It would also explain my deep shame afterwards, because it is common to feel embarrassed after having a panic attack.

It was comforting to have a reason for what had happened and why I continued to feel shame. Could the panic attack be to blame instead of Aaron? I sincerely wanted to find peace with my husband again, but I was so overwhelmed and fearful that I didn't know how to go about doing it. Knowledge alone couldn't change the fact I still felt fragile.

Other than my averted eyes and the occasional admission that adjusting to having two kids was tough, most people had no indication I was suffering. Aaron tried to talk to me, but whenever I tried to be honest, I froze up and said, "I don't know." His eyes unintentionally repelled mine like the wrong side of a magnet. The possibility of seeing his disappointment with me was too great a risk.

As the weeks went on, I got better at preparing for the certain reminders of my helplessness and loss of voice by scanning my environment for threats, particularly the threat of other people's expectations. After throwing a few verbal punches, I realized that I preferred the power I felt when angry to the helplessness I usually felt. Adrenaline-anger made me strong. And anger kept people away – especially Aaron, the most likely person to touch the black and blue inside of me.

It felt like I was the target of a deep conspiracy: *Everyone – do everything you can to make life hard for Andrea.* It didn't make sense, but it didn't have to make sense. Blaming others for my pain helped me avoid tears of vulnerability and validated my anger. After all, I had to protect myself.

My internal equilibrium was incredibly brittle, so anything unexpected felt shattering. Anyone asking something of me felt like a jab I had to dodge.

Baby waking. Supper burning. Milk spilling.

How DARE they ask anything of me! I can't take it. Make it STOP!

And so I would verbally jab back: *PLEASE go back to sleep! I'm sorry I'm such a horrible cook! Stupid dog! It's not supposed to be like this!*

My relationship with my family felt volatile and unpredictable. It's hard to feel close to others when you're convinced they're trying to sabotage your internal security. I was fighting back just to access a strength that ensured I would never be trapped in again.

Leave me alone! Pushing away was all I had.

Held hostage in my own body that was overly sensitized, and in an environment with small children who had no idea that their whining, screams and messes all bombarded my nervous system overwhelmed me emotionally. Heck, I didn't realize what the chaos was doing to me physically.

Floaters in my eyes were my first undeniable indication that something was wrong with my body. I decided to ask about them at our six-week check-up.

"What are these shadows in my eyes?" I asked the doctor. "I didn't have them before delivery and now I see them anytime I'm looking into light. They're all over – like shadows of little worms and dots."

He informed me that they were probably floaters, knocked around from delivery. I asked if they would ever go away and he said that they probably wouldn't.

"How's everything else going?" the doctor asked.

"It's been OK, but I need to apologize," I stated as though it were a matter of fact.

"What do you mean?"

In spite of not really wanting to discuss it, my masters degree in counseling created a sense of professional responsibility to let him know what had happened and to salvage whatever respect he might still have for me. Surely he saw what a fool I had made of myself. "Well, I want to apologize for freaking out during labor."

He tilted his head and leaned in, "What do you mean? I thought you did great."

"Well, you must not have been there for the worst of it then. I talked to a psychologist friend of mine, and he said I probably had a panic attack during labor. Having never had one before, I didn't know what was happening, and I was really scared." I saw his eyes open wide, "Oh – I'm fine now. I just wanted to apologize, and let you know."

"Are you sure? Be sure to let me know if you think you might be depressed or anything."

"Oh, I'm OK. I have a counseling degree." I said, as if that excused me from being honest. My credentials made a great hiding place.

"All right." He looked unconvinced but I wasn't about to act weak or needy now. I just wanted to acknowledge how crazy I looked in labor so he would know that I was not usually like that.

Attempting to focus on the floaters wandering around in my eyes, I wondered as I left the clinic, how many other residual effects delivery had had on my body. The sights and sounds of young motherhood felt like pins poking my skin from the inside. Every request and need for me to provide something felt like added pressure. It was like I was under attack, and I used my voice to try to stop it. The kids, of course, were doing things no differently than any other infant and two-year-old. But I was not able to handle it with patience or grace, though I thought I should.

When my husband said anything that made me believe I was displeasing him in any way, I snapped back. He had to be silenced, so he wouldn't stir up the fear I kept shoving away, the fear that I was a huge disappointment to him.

My relational interactions with my husband and children were more irritable than I ever wanted them to be. It had very little to do with them and a lot to do with the trauma I lived over and over when inundating sensations bombarded my frayed nerves. Previously a little sensitive, now my sensory radar was particularly overstimulated after childbirth. Absorbing every sight, sound, touch, taste and smell that came my way, I lived overwhelmed.

Without intending to dominate those around me or deliberately to make them feel belittled or under my control, I used my voice to silence others in an effort to still the overwhelming storm inside of me.

CHAPTER 26

Figuring out over time that my fears were irrational meant very little when my heart and instinctive reactions screamed something totally different. Simply adjusting the outside of me could not bring genuine, lasting change. Deeper issues of the heart needed to be addressed for powerful, lasting transformation in my voice. The weight of the "shoulds" haunted me, leaving me cowering.

I should have handled it better.
I should have been prepared.
I should have more to give.
I should get more done.
I should be happier.
I should be kind.
I should pray.

But I couldn't pray. And I wasn't sure I wanted to.

Praying evoked some sort of awareness of God's presence and I didn't want my heart to be in *anyone's* presence. It's hard to want to be around anyone when you feel disgraced. I felt I had failed this natural birth thing. Rather than overcoming and feeling empowered like some women do, I felt dragged, beaten, terrified, and discarded.

My "shoulds" covered me in shame so all I wanted to do was hide. I didn't want to be near any person – much less God. Insurmountable feeling trumped my ability to reason my way through this.

During long talks with my sister-in-law Kili, who was a spiritual director, I realized that my struggle was not just about Aaron. It was about God too.

One evening, while cleaning up supper in her kitchen, she asked how things were going with Uprising. "It amazes me, Kili." I shook my head, "But it's going really well. We have a good plan for the coming year so we can start to include college men. I'm excited about it."

"That's wonderful! You do such a great job connecting with those young women. What do you think Uprising could become? Is this something you'll do for a long time?" she wondered.

"I'm not sure. I totally love it, and I love the girls. But I've also told them I feel like in a way they're guinea pigs. It's like I'm trying out teaching styles, conversations and leadership things on them. I feel like there's something bigger to come."

"Like what?"

"I don't know. I'd like to write, but I'm not sure how to do that. I feel like there's something important for me to do or say, but I need to be… this is going to sound weird…but it seems like I need to be purified first. Like I'm not quite ready for it."

As always, Kili leaned in and continued to be curious about my heart like the friend I'd always wanted since elementary school. "What does it feel like needs to be purified?"

I confessed to her, "I can't look Aaron in the eyes. It's been months since I had Grant, but I still can't even look at my husband."

"Really? What are you afraid you'll see?"

I let out a little sob and admitted, "Disgust. Although I know Aaron would never leave me, I'm scared to death that he won't ever really love me again."

Her eyes seemed to see all the way down to my soul. "How does Aaron respond to you?"

"Whenever I'm sad or upset, he just gets irritated. I'd rather just hide from him than make him even more annoyed with me. I feel like he can't handle all my emotion." I paused as I thought about it more, "Before I got married, I was a pretty confident person. But since getting married, my confidence goes up and down all the time. Mostly down now."

Kili walked over to the counter where I sat. "How does God seem to feel about all of this, Andrea??" she wondered.

A few seconds passed as I pondered how I'd been hiding from God. "Actually, when I think about it, I'm not sure. It's like God is here, but I can't look Him. I'm so afraid that He is shaking His head as He looks on me that I can't bring myself to look at Him either. When I do lift my gaze, all I see is His profile. Maybe He isn't only shaking His head at me, maybe He isn't even looking."

Maybe He turned His head when I called out to Him in labor and doesn't plan on turning back. What's the point of talking to a god who doesn't see me? It's humiliating.

Could I live out what I said I believed? It was as if I had failed and couldn't make up for it, so I hid, not wanting anyone to see me like that. Whose expectations was I concerned about, anyway? I spent a lot of time comparing myself to my old ideal self – the Andrea I always thought I could be: good, strong and competent.

This time my need to be ideal was set in a new context. Although I finally had great husband, kids and a meaningful ministry with college women, now it seemed like I didn't deserve it. When the ideal wife-mother Andrea unraveled - completely, this time - I didn't know who I was or how to hold it together. Not only was I worried about losing other people's respect, I'd lost my self-respect. Maybe I didn't deserve respect at all.

In my daily interactions, I *demanded* peace on my own terms. I gave off the message, "Invade my territory, and you'll regret it." If I sensed pressure of any kind, I fought to relieve it.

At the time, I had a job teaching Bible classes at Horizon Counseling and Recovery Center. The class gave me an opportunity to be around other people who knew exactly what it meant to bottom out and then lean heavily on God and community to help regain their footing. I felt a camaraderie with the men with whom I worked. They were hungry to live into the forgiveness and freedom they'd experienced or were seeking. I was no more than a companion-guide on their journey. For one hour a week, we were in this forgiveness-seeking, grace-living quest together. I heard their painful, sad stories and then rejoiced with them in the freedom they were currently experiencing since being completely shattered and finding God. It gave me hope for myself. Maybe I would live in freedom again someday too.

Bottoming out was one of the most painful things I could imagine a person experiencing. It was not simply brokenness; it was finding that nightmares had come true.

There are certainly more physically painful experiences than back labor and more emotionally painful losses than being treated like a child. But when I felt trapped externally and my voice felt silenced on the inside, I wanted to die because I didn't believe I could handle the physical or the emotional pain. I'd lost the thing I'd always counted on to come through for me. I'd lost the thing that for years I'd poured strategy and energy into to ensuring I would never lose. I had lost my voice.

The turmoil and relational tension in the delivery room stripped my voice from me. Or maybe I surrendered it? I certainly felt like a victim instead of an agent in my own labor and delivery experience. I was a mess.

One of my greatest desires was to have a voice in the greater dialogue of life. So my greatest fear was that I would lose the respect of others and therefore not have a voice.

Surely God is disappointed with me. Surely he doesn't want to hear what I have to say. I'm not sure I want to hear what I have to say. It seems that everything I say is a jumbled up mess of chaos, anyway.

It took a while for me to come to terms with the fact that without getting help, I would miss out on enjoying the beautiful gift of my precious family and possibly even damage them more. Even though it would mean walking right into everything I feared, the hearts of my family members were worth it. And my heart was worth it.

CHAPTER 27

It was time to deal with the fear that had stripped me of my voice. And I knew exactly where I needed to go. Rather than avoiding the stormy mess of my heart, I needed to enter it.

Eighteen months after my heart froze, I escaped from the day-to-day grind of my own life and found Dr. Larry Crabb with a roomful of classmates in Colorado Springs. For ten years I had considered him to be my literary mentor, but I needed more than books this time. In addition to needing intervention, I desired personal validation. I believed I needed to feel better about myself before bitterness took over my heart. His class on spiritual direction offered to help train me in the art of listening to and journeying with people as they seek to deepen their relationship with God. I came to the week-long class ready to explore my own relationship with God and to receive whatever He had for me there.

On the second day of classes, Dr. Crabb said something off-the-cuff in the middle of class that made me cringe with conviction: "If you say that 'the only way I feel good is if my husband validates me,' you're a leech."

For two seconds, I blinked away tears before they began to gush. The blunt words ripped down through the layer of ice around my heart, releasing my deep grief. Rushing to my room, I fell face forward on my bed. With no one around, I honestly poured out my feelings to God.

"That's me, God. I know it. I know I'm sucking the life out of my husband because I so desperately want his validation. But I haven't known what to do. I can't trust him with my heart. He shook his head at me, God! In my most vulnerable moment, it seemed my husband abandoned and even hated me. How can I be OK with that? Don't I deserve to have him validate me? I waited forever for him. How could he turn his back on me?"

For a moment I fell silent, resting my forehead on the bed as I continued to lie there. Then a new wave of grief overcame me.

"WHERE WERE YOU?!" I hit the bed with my fist. *"Where WERE You when I was so scared? Why didn't You come and save me from my pain when I asked? What good is it to be close to You if You don't answer me when I call?"*

"I was trapped! I had nowhere to go and no one would help me. But God, YOU didn't help me either. How did You expect me to respond to Your silence?"

"Were You embarrassed by me, too? Were You shaking Your head and rolling Your eyes at me as I screamed that I didn't want to go on?" My arms curled up between my body and the bed. *"YOU EMBARRASSED ME by leaving me hanging when I called Your name! How can I look in Your eyes when I can't trust You?"*

I panted in a decrescendo, like I'd just given birth to the grief that had been growing inside of me for a year and a half. An image of Aaron sitting on a throne flashed in my mind.

I've made Aaron my idol! I've been relying on his love and respect to validate me! I am a leech!

I had come to beat on God's chest, and, rather than pushing me away, He had let me feel the fear and shame that was about to devour me. And then He had rescued me from it.

In that moment, I felt the arms of God surrounding as I wept into the green nylon bedspread. I sensed His voice saying that He forgave me, loved me and that He was with me all along.

"I'm so sorry, God. I have been looking to Aaron to make me feel loved and valuable instead of trusting You to do that for me. I demanded that he adore me so I could feel good about myself. But I don't want to live like that. I don't want to put pressure on him to do for me what only You can do. Forgive me for putting him on the throne of my heart where You belong. You're the only One Who can love me perfectly. Thank You for loving me even when I treat You like this. I'm ready to move on."

Peace warmed my heart as I voiced my revelation to God, looking Him right in the eye. *"You were with me. You felt compassion for me in my pain. I don't know why You didn't rescue me from it, but You were there. I know now."*

Looking at my own heart, the realization dawned that the pain and embarrassment could not destroy me unless I let it. My heart was alive and secure, and I knew I was going to be OK. From now on, I wasn't going to rely on another person to prove to me I was loved or worthy of love anymore. Instead, I could rely on the unchanging and sacrificial love of God for that.

After living for so long to nurse an open wound, I'd never dealt with the source of my pain. I didn't need any more bandages; I needed surgery. The tears I cried on that bed in Colorado Springs were tears of deep sadness over the realization that I had been hurting Aaron and our kids by transferring my own anxiety onto them.

My worst nightmare had come true. I was too much for my family. Too much demand. Too much shame. Too much pressure.

But after my conversation with God, I was able to see again. Fear did not blind me anymore. Opening my heart, I raised my eyes off of myself and began looking around at the rubble. For the first time,

I was able to see the truth about my husband. I was not the only one who went through my own worst nightmare in childbirth. He did too. The pressure we took on to be the "perfect little family" had crushed us with what felt like failure.

It had to have been difficult for Aaron to see me suffering so much pain and to feel completely disempowered. He might have been embarrassed, but maybe that was because he was looking for validation, too. We had both felt trapped and scared. And rather than turning toward one another, we had turned away from each other.

Once my heart felt secure, I could lift my eyes off of myself and see Aaron more clearly. His heart had been wounded like mine, and then I had continued to hurt him even more. For months I had shut him out and refused to accept the love and care that he attempted to offer to me. I had closed my heart to my husband even after I knew my ongoing pain had more to do with my body's response to the trauma than anything Aaron did or didn't do.

Rolling over on the bed, I looked up at the ceiling. Realizing that my intention would be difficult to follow up with action, I determined then and there that I wanted to demonstrate my love for my husband regardless of his response to me.

Stirred by the discussions in our School of Spiritual Direction class, the vision of expressing the self-giving, proactive and invitational love of God to my husband was able to transcend my own fear. It was time to stop being defensive and to begin acknowledging how, by holding back and protecting myself from the possibility of more pain, I had actually hurt myself and others more.

Throwing up my hands to defend the ideal-wife Andrea wasn't necessary anymore. No, I wanted to be the real-wife Andrea, who is forgiven for her faults and empowered when she acknowledges her weaknesses. I wanted to see clearly in order to accept my own beauty and strength and to stand in the way of and absorb the impact of fear, shame and pressure that threatened my family.

Calling Aaron, I told him I had much to share with him. If we had been magnets repelling one another for so many months, my confession and acceptance of God's forgiveness seemed to flip me around so that now I couldn't get to Aaron fast enough. As soon as I returned home, I read a letter out loud to Aaron.

> *I have a much different perspective on the traumatic moment and months that followed 17 months ago. If it hadn't happened, I may have not realized the intensity to which I have looked to you to fill the deepest longings of my heart – and I may have gone on like that for years...I long to invite you into a relationship with me that is characterized, not by expectation, but by loving self-sacrifice. I want to explore what it means to open myself to you and receive from you where I have previously been closed. I am bursting with longing to love you freely and without demand.*

From this perspective, I was able to see the mercy of our shattering experience. We had been suffering under shame and pressure to perform for one another. I didn't want to live like that anymore. Neither did he.

The freedom in our marriage that followed was more than I could imagine. It took us both a little while to get used to relating to one another differently when we had arguments or when we felt offended by one another. It was like a muscle that needed to be built up and consistently trained to maintain. It was hard to break out of the offense vs. defense game when we'd been playing it for so long. We certainly continued to have our moments of disagreement. However, the tension that used to last for days and was never quite released, now began to evaporate in minutes.

In spite of feeling more vulnerable to experiencing pain, I was more able to handle the pain with confidence. It was incredibly empowering.

"I know now, God. My heart is secure, even indestructible. I don't need to feel pressure and shame if I'm not relying on a person to love me. If You love me, I am free to love others no matter how they feel about me. Let's do this."

CHAPTER 28

The day after I got back from Colorado Springs, Aaron and I decided to move our family to a new town. He would have the opportunity to put his physical therapy and leadership skills to good use as an owner in a young clinic, and he wanted to provide abundantly for our family so that I could focus on whatever ministry we pursued. I felt incredibly blessed by his belief in me.

The move was not a decision we took lightly. We would be moving away from dear family. Three-year old Amelia was worried she would have to leave her tricycle. Aaron was concerned because he knew I would have to leave Uprising.

Telling the girls that we were moving was one of the hardest things I'd ever done. There was an unusually small group of girls in our basement that November night. I had everyone sit in a circle on the floor so I could have them close to me when I broke the news. I knew it would be a completely unexpected announcement, which concerned me. I knew what it felt like to be taken by surprise.

"I need to tell you guys something. One of the hardest things for me is to know my husband is feeling stifled. I see so much potential in him to make a big difference, but it's hard to be all he can be in the position he's in now. As hard as it is to say this, we have decided to move to

North Platte where Aaron can be an owner in a clinic."

The girls were silent until one spoke up, "How soon will you move?"

"Well, this is also difficult to tell you, but Aaron starts in North Platte on December 1st. We are putting our house on the market tomorrow and will move as soon as possible." Tears started to form in the wide eyes of those in the circle. "I'm so sorry, guys. Aaron even questioned if we should leave Uprising. He loves you guys and believes in what we're doing here. But we agreed that this is what we need to do."

I began to speak with passion behind my tears, "I love you guys so much. You are so important to me, and I know that what we have here is something really special. And the truth is, each of you will graduate someday soon, move away, and begin a life outside of Uprising. This kind of love in community is hard to find, and I can't promise that you'll have it again quite like this. But I can promise you this, if there is anything I've learned, it is that we cannot rely on the love of other people to sustain us. People will come and go. It is only the love of the Lord that endures."

I reached behind me and pressed play on a CD I had ready. Dark, yet hopeful tones encircled us when I turned the music up as Joy Williams began to sing "The Love of the Lord Endures." Joining her in singing with conviction, I took the hands of the girls next to me, and we formed a circle of tearful connection.

It was only a couple of weeks later when the circle had to be broken. Although we were confident in our decision to move, both Aaron and I felt sad to leave the young women who had become part of our family. We knew that whatever came next, it wouldn't be the same. It couldn't be. Transitions like these were difficult.

As we prepared to leave, I thought about all of the difficult conversations. The confessions. The connection. Did I handle them well? What should I have done differently? Did I set them up for disillusionment by pouring so much into them and then leaving them so suddenly? I loved these women like sisters. I believed in them. We had connected with each other, and we had kept moving forward even when things got tough. Until it was time for Aaron and me to leave.

In the months that followed, we all missed the intimate connection we had shared on Thursday nights. Eventually, I learned that the core group I had thought would support one another had dispersed. Hardly any of them spent time together, let alone made the effort to connect deeply.

It was difficult to understand. Hadn't we built lasting connections together? What went wrong? As the common denominator in the group, I had poured my heart out and invited them to pour out theirs. In creating the environment, had I set them up to be overly dependent on me?

The most impactful ministry experience of my life sputtered out and left people deeply wounded. What could I have done in the transition to empower them more fully for the change to come? I firmly believed that the deep connection forged in authenticity was worth the inevitable mess that real relationships made, but I began to wonder if I were in over my head when I guided others into it. Maybe I was playing with fire. *Maybe I should back off.*

At first, the move to our new town was exciting. There were many decisions to be made and so much to learn about owning a business. However, it didn't take long before it felt like we were fighting to stay afloat. Aaron worked long hours, and when he wasn't working, he was discussing the business with me.

Amelia was three, and Grant was one, so I was in the thick of mothering small children who needed me all of the time. With a busy husband, few friends and no idea what to do with my young children in the wintertime, I spiraled down again. My mind was a menace. With no time or energy to intently process anything, I was left feeling like every thought, emotion and experience was trapped inside my pressure-cooker of a head.

Why can't I find more meaning in carrying out my family responsibilities? It's not fair that I can't sleep! Walking around like a frustrated zombie being prodded by expectation, I could only imagine how frightening that picture was to a couple of sweet but needy little kiddos.

In conversations with my husband, I was taking more risks. In fact, we were doing pretty well. But it still felt like there was very little connection between me and God.

The day-to-day meeting of the kids' physical and emotional needs overwhelmed me. Getting up for every feeding, nightmare, and thirst made it very difficult for me to be rested. My frayed nerves again left me feeling as if I had needles poking my skin from the inside.

My senses were overloaded by loud, whiny tears, barking dogs, chaotic clutter, and bright lights. But it wasn't the sensory stimulation that was causing me the most difficulty; it was my reaction to it. Rather than recognizing it for what it was and dealing with it as a physical problem, I began to question my own emotional stability and spiritual maturity.

I should be able to handle this. There is something wrong with me! What is wrong with me? Why am I so angry? I'm so angry all the time!

My inner dialogue became a running list of ways that I was failing my family. It was self-loathing, self-pitying self-talk, strangling me in my own shame and fear. My internal pressure elevated as the external expectations pressed in on me. Anxiety begged my self-protection to take over. I anticipated the impending *pop* with great fear. I didn't want to explode.

It took a trusted friend to draw a line in the sand and invite me out of my hole. Almost 2 1/2 years after Grant's birth, a close high school friend was back for her grandmother's funeral. She invited me to visit in the most private place we could think of so that we could talk one-on-one with no kids around.

We sat on the only furniture left in her late-grandma's dimly lit nursing home room. Life-lived poignancy struck me. It was the perfect place to have a life-living conversation. This is how I remember it:

"Are you depressed? Do you enjoy your kids?" she asked.

"Well…I love them," I mused. "And there are moments I enjoy them, but most of the time I feel frustrated by all their needs that I am expected to meet. But I'm their mom. Isn't that my job?"

"Do you want to be angry at your kids, or will you look back on this time of your life and wish you had been able to enjoy it?"

There's nothing like end-of-life reminders to evoke right-now-life movement. Her question made me realize I didn't want to live to survive; I wanted to live a life of deep joy alongside whatever pain would come. But I could not do it on my own.

Soon after our conversation, I began taking anti-depressants. My goal was to use them to help me regain chemical balance in my brain while I continued to work on my health and rekindle my connection with God. It was in taking the antidepressants that I realized how truly sensitive I was. The medication took the edge off of my sensory perception, and I felt a much stronger buffer between me and the sensory world of sights, sounds, tastes, smells and touch. It felt as though I were on the outside looking in at the world again. While I appreciated the fact that I had more control over my emotional expression, honestly, the buffer was so strong that I started to miss my sensitivity.

I determined to give my brain a chance to recover so I could break out of the intense sensitivity and start making choices to create a buffer naturally. Several months later, I went off of the medication and transitioned into a new awareness of how the choices I made daily impacted my natural buffer, which had big repercussions on my spiritual and mental health.

After researching emotional intensity and sensitivity, I began to treat my overstimulation as a physical ailment rather than a spiritual deficiency or a deep conspiracy by the outside world. Whenever I realized that my internal dialogue ran through my failures, I stopped and asked, *What is impacting my senses right now?* And I began to recognize that a lack of sleep, hormonal cycles, and noise were the problem, not the state of my heart. But God still felt far away.

Hesitantly, I began a small group with other moms of young kids in hopes that I could connect with people and my passion. Maybe it would help me feel more connected to God again. After meeting with a handful of friends for a few months, I spoke for a Mothers of Preschoolers group about self-protection and my experience of childbirth and postpartum depression. It felt good to be using my voice in the world again, a year after leaving Uprising. But was anything I said making any difference?

Then I hosted a little Christmas gathering for my MOPS small group. Only one person came, and I didn't know her. She quietly sat with her head tilted down and her shoulders pulled in to her chest. I wondered if we would actually talk or if we would sit in awkward silence as our toddlers played at our feet.

Then she spoke up. "You know when you spoke at MOPS? I've never heard anyone say anything as honest as what you said," she commented. "I don't have friends. Actually, the first time I came to MOPS, I was so nervous that I almost walked back out. But someone caught me and convinced me to stay. I'm really glad I did. I'm really glad I got to hear your talk."

For the next hour, she shared stories of her life that revealed an incredible inner strength and beauty she didn't realize she possessed. I was awed and inspired by her transparency. We continued to meet regularly for months. She amazed me over and over as she made new friends, shared her story with our small group and began to grow outwardly into the woman that she was on the inside. She had found the voice of her heart, and ,with time and repetition, she began to use it with great power.

Maybe when I use my voice it inspires others to use theirs. Yet whenever considering the possibilities of speaking or writing, I questioned what I said more than ever.

What if I say something and I offend others? What if I say something and then people disagree with me? Will they completely write me off? Is speaking up worth the risk?

I longed for a resolution to my questions. I yearned to use my voice for a bigger purpose. Deep-seated belief kept whispering to me.

Don't give up...Wait for it...

CHAPTER 29

In the spring of 2012, I attended a follow-up class with Dr. Larry Crabb. My relational interactions with Aaron had improved dramatically since attending the first class. We felt more connected and free than we ever had before. But I continued to struggle with how to release my true self in the world, beyond my close relationships. In spite of trying to convince myself that I shouldn't want the opportunity to speak on a bigger stage, I couldn't shake my childhood desire to sing the song in my heart and to contribute to broader discussions. I still felt as though there were something in me that I was supposed to discuss with the outside world. But who would listen?

There was an image in my head of a ladder, much like the ladder of success. But this ladder was the ladder of respect. It felt as though I was supposed to climb the ladder and earn my way to the top. If I could do that, someone important might notice me and give me an opportunity to speak or write in order to make the difference I longed to make.

It was a game I had played my whole life, one where I felt I needed to prove myself to be heard. But I didn't want to play anymore. No one could truly win.

Besides, how do I know I'm really doing what God wants me to do, anyway? I don't feel His presence like I used to. It feels like He is so far away. Maybe I don't have the right to speak if my relationship with God seems distant. When will my heart ever be in the right place to really offer my gifts?

The week of class was almost over when Dr. Crabb stood up front with his overhead projector and declared that he wanted to share the vision of what "Kingdom relating" might look like. I sat in the back center of the room, opened my notebook and began writing as he spoke.

Larry drew out a diagram on his overhead projector. In it, he described how God interacts with people, and he connected that kind of relating with how people could interact with others. If we are to model our behavior after God's behavior, then it made sense to imitate how he interacts with people.

There in the back row, my pen nearly burned through my paper as I took notes. My leg bounced under the table in increasing intensity as I leaned over my notebook, then looked up to the diagram Larry continued to describe.

"It's nice to feel close to God, but the fact is that we don't always feel close to God. If you want to really experience God, express Him! Express His loving character as a God who invites people to Himself and moves into the chaos of a hurting world."

The energy from my bouncing leg started vibrating through my entire being until I could contain my excitement no longer. Larry concluded and flipped his overhead projector switch off. I put down my pen and nearly crawled over the legs of the person sitting next to me in order to reach the aisle.

"Hey Andrea. I've got a...." Someone tried to catch me, but in that moment, I was on a mission.

I raised my finger, "I'll be back in a sec."

I turned and nearly ran up the short aisle. I had to catch Larry before anyone else could corner him and press the moment away.

"Larry…" I stood in front of the author who had taught me what it meant to connect deeply with other people and to see shattered dreams as an opportunity to know God more intimately by expressing His love sacrificially, the man whose books resonated in my entire being and made me believe I wasn't alone.

Grabbing his arms, I declared with lips trembling in conviction. "THIS! THIS I can live for!" Then I threw my arms around him. "Thank you!"

Any other response would have been disingenuous. There was no need for others to respect me, no demand to be heard. Tears dampened my cheeks in one of the most honest and loving expressions of myself that I'd ever shown.

"You're welcome," Larry smiled, then looked at the class. "Now, THIS is Kingdom relating."

I had believed I needed to feel connected to God to really experience Him, but when I heard Larry describe God's sacrificial love, I knew everything I ever needed to know.

Jesus loves me. So I can love everyone else. I don't need them to like me. I don't need to try to earn their respect. I can sacrifice respect if I need to. I can put my reputation on the line, if necessary. I can risk everything to show the kind of love Jesus has for me.

Yes! I don't have to play games, fight or climb some silly ladder of respect to use my voice. Games and battles are for winners and losers. I don't want to be either one. I don't want to have to choose a side anymore. I want to give my voice in all its fullness as an offering poured out for others. Not against them. I want to stand in between the fear that threatens to destroy women and their voice and embrace those who do so for me as well.

It was time to reject the shame that had lured the real me into hiding. I wanted to throw off the pressure that assumed I'm best when I'm the ideal me. By opening up and inviting others to see my humanity and my beauty, I wanted to declare that God loves me just as I am because I want them to know that they also are loved. No more numbing my pain and diminishing my desire! Instead, I wanted to feel every bit of it so I could acknowledge how much I long for a perfect loving connection with God as He comforts me in my pain and fills my longing.

I am free when I am not bound by fear.
I am free when I am able to risk internal safety for someone else.
I am free when I do not get defensive when I'm accused.
I am free when I do not close myself to love!
I am free when I feel my pain honestly and accept comfort.

As I heard Larry wrap up his lecture, I couldn't stop thinking about my life: "Healing isn't being pain free. True healing is when you love, despite the pain."

Yes! Loving like that is worth the risk of losing my connection and impact with others. It's not about me!

A few days after I got home, I went back to Hastings to attend the senior art exhibit for Christi, a young woman still in my heart. It had been two and a half years since I had told the Uprising girls goodbye. I sat in the audience, humbled and yet thrilled as I could be, as she began describing her project.

> *"The story I told in Senior Thesis begins in September, 2008. It was my first month at college, and I found myself on a women's retreat. The woman leading the retreat was reading and teaching from Genesis 3. Adam and Eve had just eaten of the fruit that God commanded them not to. After disobeying God, they heard the familiar sound of God walking in the garden, and they hid from Him in shame. God calls to them, "Where are you?" Reading this as a child left me confused....I saw that God has just been betrayed, and He's about to curse the world - He must be mad.*

This misunderstanding twisted God's character in my perception and left me confused until 2008, the retreat. As the woman leading read through this passage, she began crying and voiced God as burdened and broken. In that moment, I understood. Perfect companionship with His beloved was lost; there was sorrow due to separation. When I saw more clearly God's response to the Fall, it revealed God's own love to my sight. The simple truth of God's unfailing love change me that day; I have never been the same."

The same young freshman at the retreat four years before who was so amazed that God actually loved her was displaying her Senior Thesis exhibit of painted images answering God's question: "Where are you? Where is your heart?"

The weight and reality of the moment compelled me to proceed meditatively into her exhibit. Eleven large paintings lined the walls, each an outward representation of an inward reality Christi had experienced. There were women dancing, hiding, crumbling and seeking. I was in awe of how beautifully she represented so many states of the heart, conditions that I, too, knew well.

Turning a corner, I froze. Time stood still as I stood weeping. On the wall before me hung a painting of a woman in a soft white dress, leaping off a cliff with nothing but darkness below. But the woman in white wasn't scared or timid. This woman's arms spread wide from her sides, and her position in the air made it clear that she hadn't been pushed off the cliff. She had taken the leap confidently.

I couldn't believe my eyes. A quote Larry Crabb had paraphrased from C.S. Lewis gripped me. It described what it meant to trust in the "rope" of God's love: "You never know how much you believe in the strength of a rope until you jump off a cliff."[5] And here I was in the middle of Christi's art show, staring at a picture illustrating my hearts reality ever since running up the aisle and giving Larry that hug. I had an overwhelming sense that the painting was for me.

After tearfully explaining my reaction to Christi, I turned to view the rest of the art show, which included the work of another young woman. The other artist constructed dresses out of items she found in nature. One was grand, made of long branches that bent at the ground and extended out in an over six-foot radius. It was beautiful, but the spiky ends were intimidating, as though they were intentionally keeping anyone from getting too close.

What would it be like to be a child whose mother wore this dress? How would her children ever approach her?

My tears began to flow again as I realized that there were times when I wore such an unapproachable presence with my own children. I stood there in the middle of the art exhibit, the dress of self-protection on one side and the leap of vulnerable love on the other. What would I choose? For many years, my mama-heart's answer to the question "Where are you?" was the dress of self-protection. But I didn't want to wear it anymore.

I want to be the woman in soft white dress. I want to trust God with my heart and take big, cliff-jumping risks. It was time to display extraordinary love.

CHAPTER 30

How could I use my voice in the outside world when I was frustrated by everything that overwhelmed my head and heart? It wasn't that I was unwilling to be authentic at this point. I was simply concerned that I wouldn't ever be able to express myself clearly to others. What good are creative ideas and fascinating connections if I can't articulate them outside of my own head?

"I don't want to waste what you've given me, God. Help me know how to communicate clearly."

It was as if every experience, idea, feeling and bit of knowledge or theology were little dots, all connected together in my brain. I couldn't talk about one without going down a dozen other paths and ending up confusing my conversation partner. If I tried to pull one dot out to talk about it, a bunch of other dots followed. My head felt like a tangled web of abstract confusion with no way to convey it clearly. Not only that, but I was also still exhausted as a mom of young children. I found it particularly difficult to think and speak clearly when fatigue clouded my mind.

However, music, books, movies and visual arts spoke to me in ways that simple statements or teachings never could. Artistic expressions had the ability to connect disparaging points, subtext and the constant flow of concepts in my mind and turn them into something beautiful. Still, I never expected a Disney movie to be the key that would unlock my message and help me release my voice.

On November 30, 2013, I watched my life flash before my eyes in a stunning parable on the screen. My experience watching *Frozen* completely undid me. I related intimately to the snow queen Elsa and the painful journey that led her to conceal her powers, rather than feel the intensity of her emotions, and to do everything she could to keep from showing it all to the world. Eventually the whole kingdom found out she had the power to release snow and ice from her extremities, so she ran away and up a mountain where she could be who she was without harming anyone else.

I couldn't believe my eyes and ears. I knew exactly what Elsa experienced. It seemed she struggled with her powers like I had struggled with mine. Like Elsa, I had also tried to be what I had assumed everyone wanted of me, to conceal the depth of my thoughts, to numb the intensity of my feelings and certainly not to let them show so expressively. It amused me that Elsa had accidentally exposed herself by releasing ice when she felt overwhelmed at her own coronation. Seminary was a far cry from a crowning event, but my experience there had begun with my own accidental exposure of my feelings for Shane. Elsa had revealed the fact she was super human. I had revealed the fact I was only human, with longing and weakness just like everyone else.

When I watched her experiment with her powers on the mountain while singing "Let It Go," something inside me awakened my own longing to sing again. Not to sing children's songs to my kids, but big, emotionally honest, grown-up ones. There had been no particular song in my heart for so many years that I had forgotten what it felt like to let a song out spontaneously.

It also amazed me how accurately Elsa expressed my own experience with being overwhelmed by pressured expectations. She consistently turned her back, closed her eyes and shook her head in an attempt to hold back the frustration and fear that welled up inside of her. But just as the people I loved didn't have any idea what I needed in those moments, Elsa's sweet sister Anna didn't either. Anna pushed Elsa over the edge with her insistence, time and time again. And just as I would explode with bursts of frustration on my family, Elsa exploded with ice.

But it wasn't only Elsa to whom I could relate to. Anna had her own journey. The girls' parents had secluded them both as they grew up, but Anna didn't know why. She longed to feel connected to someone because her sister continuously shut her out. And that longing had made her search for love and validation from a man. I too had looked for a man to validate my identity and my voice.

Then when Elsa struck Anna's heart with ice, Anna began to freeze from the inside-out. She and her companions asked advice and learned that the only thing that could thaw a frozen heart was an act of true love. They assumed Anna needed "true love's kiss" to be saved.

The whole scenario gripped me. What did it mean that Elsa struck Anna's heart with ice? Anna had pursued Elsa all the way up a treacherous path to the top of a mountain only to be rejected by her sister. The one thing she had always wanted was to connect with Elsa, but instead, in Anna's greatest moment of vulnerability, after pursuing and defending her sister, Elsa rejected her.

Perhaps the ice that struck Anna's heart was rejection, and her heart's freezing reaction was fear and bitterness. It was at the point of "true love's kiss" that I departed from relating to *Frozen*.

I knew no man would be able to convince Anna she was loved. I knew that if she needed "true love's kiss" to validate her, she was a leech.

But the movie took a turn I didn't expect. Just when Anna was about to freeze, she had a choice to make. Would she run to the man who could save her or would she run to save her sister who was about to be struck by the sword of the villain?

Anna ran to her sister and threw her hand up to the sword that intended to destroy Elsa. And just before it struck her, she turned to solid ice.

Amazing! Anna chose sacrificial love over waiting for someone to convince her she was loved! She chose to give herself for her sister instead of protecting herself. She chose to love, despite the pain.

Then, moments later, she began to thaw. Olaf previously demonstrated his willingness to melt to save Anna, so perhaps the knowledge that she was loved that much freed her from pursuing further validation and released her to express her love for her sister. Anna's act of true love saved her! She experienced true healing – not an absence of pain, but rather the act of loving despite her pain. Anna acted on love instead of waiting for it!

Elsa's nightmare came true, and her sister still loved her. In that moment, she knew that it was fear that had turned her powers into a destructive force and it was love that could turn them into a beautiful gift to the world.

It was breath-taking. The entire movie played out before me as though the filmmakers had intended to turn my life into their movie.

However, one scene remained. The kingdom gathered in Anna and Elsa's castle courtyard, and with a little smile, Elsa asked, "Are you ready?" Then she unapologetically used her powers to enrich the lives of the people around her by creating an ice rink and ice sculptures for them to enjoy. She didn't hide her gift. She didn't pretend that she didn't care. She shared her gift in a beautiful display of loving self-expression to meet the real needs of people around her.

I had cried throughout the whole movie; but, at that point, I sobbed as I heard another whisper to my spirit say: "This is the scene you have yet to play out, Andrea. It's time."

I had the *Frozen* soundtrack downloaded by the time the kids and I left the theater parking lot.

"Why are you crying so much, Mom?" Amelia wanted to know.

"I just loved the movie so much!" I didn't know how to explain it.

We scurried into our big, empty kitchen, and I plugged my phone into the speaker and filled the room with "For the First Time In Forever," "Let It Go," and the rest of the soundtrack.

I grabbed Amelia and Grant's hands, and we all attempted to sing along while waving our arms and bodies dramatically. Aaron came into the kitchen from his office to see our passionate display. "How was the movie?" he gawked.

I glided over to him with big tears in my eyes and gave him a hug. "It was...amazing."

His eyes sparkled with amusement. "Well, good!"

With song after song, the kids and I sang and danced our little dramatic hearts out, filling our big kitchen with love. Aaron even joined in the party. As I danced and sang, I realized that I'd never really shown my kids this side of me before. I hadn't been myself for so long.

Frozen reminded me who I was. It also reminded me of who I could be.

We played the soundtrack over and over. For weeks, I cried whenever the songs played. I managed to see the movie five times in the movie theater. One of those times was Christmas Day. Aaron and I rode to the theater separately from my parents, sister and the children. On the way home, I could hold it in no longer.

Emotion spilled out of my eyes and lips, "Do you see why the movie is such a big deal to me?"

"I think I do, but why don't you explain it to me?" he answered.

"I feel like Elsa. I feel like I have been hiding under the radar with my gifts for a long time because I was too much for everyone. But I don't want to hide anymore. I feel like..." I wasn't sure if I should admit what I felt, but I did anyway. "I feel like I am supposed to do something big, something extraordinary. And when I saw that last scene where Elsa offers her gift to the world in love, I sensed that God was calling me to play out that scene."

I continued through a fresh wave of tears: "I'm scared out of my mind to offer myself to the world. What if I'm rejected? Or ignored? What if what I offer isn't any good? But I can't shake the feeling that God seems to be inviting me out of hiding through this movie. It feels like it's time."

Our truck rolled into the garage, and Aaron put it into park. I needed some kind of response from him. I wanted to know that he would support me if I turned the key and released the real me to the world. "What do you think?"

He looked at me gently and then firmly stated, "I think you should 'let it go'."

EPILOGUE

One crisp morning in November, 2014, almost a year after I took our kids to *Frozen* for the first time, I dropped Grant off at preschool and climbed back into our white caravan. A dozen times I had attempted to sit down and write my thoughts about *Frozen*, but every time I had written a paragraph or two and then frozen up, unable to complete my thoughts. They were all jumbled up inside, a chaotic mess of ideas, experiences and feelings, too interconnected for me to know what to actually say.

Lord, I desperately want to share my heart with the world. It's almost been a year since FROZEN changed my life. It feels like it's now or never.

Then a simple idea for a blog post framework swirled in my head. Maybe it didn't have to be as complicated as I was making it! I pressed my foot on the gas and rushed home to grab my computer. Ten minutes later, I was seated in a coffee shop, typing my heart out to compose my first blog post entitled, "*Frozen* Top Ten."

Dozens of comments rolled in from friends and family, confirmation that putting myself out there was worth the risk. A few days later, a friend sat me down at a little Mexican restaurant, and, over chips and salsa, she petitioned, "I think you should write a book about *Frozen*, Andrea. The world needs to hear what you have to say."

Recently, Aaron and I experienced a moment of tense interaction. The frequency of that kind of interaction had decreased dramatically after my experience at the School of Spiritual Direction, but every once in a while it still happened. I had become overwhelmed by the physical overstimulation of my nervous system, along with the pressure to keep my family happy and meet all of their needs. Aaron didn't know what to do with my cold reactions, and he began to doubt himself.

When it happened that day, I threw verbal ice at Aaron and the kids in an attempt to make it all stop. Just like Elsa. Aaron saw my icy response and backed off as if I had struck his heart.

Later, we sat down on the back porch and I apologized, but the silence was thick between us. "Do you want to talk about it?" I asked.

"What am I supposed to think when you treat me like that?" he expressed his own understandable frustration with the way I had spoken to him.

"I'm really sorry, honey." I apologized. "I was wrong to act like that. And yet I want you to know that I was feeling really overwhelmed in that moment. Sometimes it feels like there are actual needles poking my eardrums and pins sticking my skin from the inside. When I feel like that, I just want it to stop. I don't want to be unkind. There are times I need you to see past my icy exterior."

He was taking it all in, so I went on, "I hate that I have the power to destroy you. In moments like the one we experienced today, I feel out of control. Deep down, hurting you is the last thing I want to do. But when I do and you run from me or try to contain me, I get the message that I'm dangerous. And that scares me. My own power scares me. When I am in my most frightening moments, that is when I most desperately need your help."

"But when I offer to help, you act like you don't want it."

"I'm sorry, Aaron. I want to stay open to your movement toward me. Would you help me remember when I become overwhelmed like that?"

He nodded and simply stated, "Yes."

"Thank you, babe. I wish I could do it on my own, but I realize now that you can help me. I wish I could help other people know they can help each other like that."

Aaron nodded as though he understood and turned to me. "And that's why you need to write this book," he answered.

Everyone is a "fixer-upper," of course. We need each other. I've found it to be true of myself. Stress brings out the worst in us, but love nurtures what we were created to offer.

I'm not suggesting that we excuse the pain we inflict on one another. I understand why Elsa threw ice, but I don't believe hurting others is justifiable. I'm suggesting that we look past frigid exteriors and snow monster defenses to see what's really going on inside. Maybe there is a playful, loving Olaf inside that longs to be drawn out with our love.

We can do this for one another. But these acts of true love do more than absorb pain directed at the person we love. When we, in love, put our own hand up to the sword instead of waiting to hear that we are loved, we find out that we are capable of true love, even if we are hurt! As Larry Crabb says, "We experience God by expressing God," not by just saying we believe in him. And "true healing is in loving, despite the pain."

You are loved. And you make the circle of God's love for you complete when you live like you're loved. It is your act of true love that can thaw your frozen heart.

There is point before the coronation when Elsa practices holding the emblems of royalty without the cover of her gloves. She stands under the controlling gaze of her father's portrait of perfection, and she trembles, in shame and under pressure, as frost comes out of her hands. But now, in this moment as I type, my hands extend an invitation. And I do it in my living room under the portrait of the liberating surrender of the cliff-jumping woman in white.

Arise, my friend. Your voice matters.

Acknowledgements

God, thank you for Your movement in my heart and for inviting me to rely on your love. Expressing Your love to others is worth living for.

Thank you to my husband, Aaron Wenburg, for your loving sacrifice and courage in supporting me as I tell our story. You challenge me, care for me and believe in me. These are the blessings I always longed to receive. I am so glad we made it to "I love you."

Amelia and Grant, loving and being loved by you is my greatest joy. You stretch me, teach me and delight me. I long to see you live into the fullness of who you are and flourish in self-giving love. I'm so glad I get to be your mom.

My heart is forever grateful for my parents Tim and Sue Moomey and my forever-Anna, my sister, Daniele Moomey. The many unpublished chapters written of our years as a young family remind me of the magnitude of your impact on my heart. I carry your strength, your compassion, your leadership and your love with me always.

Our grandparents and families have shown us overwhelming support through our lives and in the midst of this project. Thank you to Jim and Rogene Wenburg for raising Aaron to be an amazing husband, dad and friend. Chris, Jillian, Justin, Kili, Carter and Selah, I love sharing in this creative-scientific life and family with you.

Rosanne Moore, you probably didn't know what you were getting into when I first asked you to edit my little study guide! Thank you for coaching me for months and encouraging me to tell my story. You believed in me and my story when I wanted to diminish it. Thank you for helping me find my writing voice. I am proud of what we've created.

Larry and Rachael Crabb, your message ripples through my life and my relationships. I will do my best to keep the wave flowing to others.

To the guides along my path, only a few of whom I mention in the book, I am grateful to you and your contribution to my life and this story. The wisdom and loving care you showed me still fills my heart. I love including you in the book and I wish I could include more!

To each of my friends through the years, thank you for your patience with me as I've struggled to understand myself and make sense of my identity. Your companionship taught me, molded me, encouraged me and made me believe that I had a hope and a future.

To those of you who participated in small groups with me in Holdrege, Nashville, Kearney, Chicago, LaCrosse, Hastings and North Platte, I believe in you and am grateful that I had the opportunity to share deep connection with you. Your patience with and grace for me as I explored how to interact with and lead small groups greatly influenced this book and the accompanying discussion course.

UNFROZEN intentionally focuses on stories that took place away from where we make our home, and yet it is the accumulative effect of the people at home who gave me a foundation for learning about myself, others and God. Thanks, to you all!

The account of the stories in this book are my honest, subjective perception and reflection of what I experienced. I relied heavily upon my own journals, correspondence and memories of the formative moments in my life, and I verified stories with the people involved when possible. In other instances, I changed the names.

Thank you to the UNFROZEN Launch Team! Your support, engagement and feedback helped the book take its final shape and amplify its message. Don't ever forget that your voice matters.

References

1. Larry Crabb, *Connecting: Healing for Ourselves and Our Relationships* (Nashville, TN: Word Press, 1997), xi.

2. Larry Crabb, *Shattered Dreams: God's Unexpected Pathway to Joy* (Colorado Springs, CO: Waterbrook Press, 2001), 56-57.

3. *Ibid.,* 57

4. Psalm 139:13-14 NIV

5. Larry Crabb's paraphrase of a C. S. Lewis quote from *A Grief Observed*